SCOTNOTES
Number 18

D0782943

Robert Louis Stevenson's
The Strange Case of Dr Jekyll and Mr Hyde, The Master of Ballantrae and The Ebb-Tide

Gerard Carruthers

Association for Scottish Literary Studies 2004

Acknowledgements
I would like to thank the Association for Scottish Literary Studies
Schools and Further Education Committee for their wise scrutiny
of this work, and especially Ronald Renton, Convener of the
committee, for his generous assistance, and the President of the
ASLS, Alan MacGillivray, for his strong and subtle hand in guiding
the original conception of this study-note. I am also particularly
grateful to Julie Renfrew of St Margaret's Academy, Livingston,
who kindly and helpfully read and commented on earlier drafts.

Published by
Association for Scottish Literary Studies
c/o Department of Scottish History
University of Glasgow
9 University Gardens
Glasgow G12 8QH
www.asls.org.uk

First published 2004

A CIP catalogue for this title is available from the British Library

ISBN 0 948877 56 1

Subsidised by

Typeset by Roger Booth Associates, Hassocks, West Sussex

CONTENTS

Page

SCOTNOTES

Study guides to major Scottish writers and literary texts

Produced by the Schools and Further Education Committee
of the Association for Scottish Literary Studies

Series Editors
Lorna Borrowman Smith
Ronald Renton

Editorial Board

EDITORS' FOREWORD

The *Scotnotes* booklets are a series of study guides to major Scottish writers and literary texts that are likely to be elements within literature courses. They are aimed at senior pupils in secondary schools and students in further education colleges and colleges of education. Each booklet in the series is written by a person who is not only an authority on the particular writer or text but also experienced in teaching at the relevant levels in schools or colleges. Furthermore, the editorial board, composed of members of the Schools and Further Education Committee of the Association for Scottish Literary Studies, considers the suitability of each booklet for the students in question.

For many years there has been a shortage of readily accessible critical notes for the general student of Scottish literature. *Scotnotes* has grown as a series to meet this need, and provides students with valuable aids to the understanding and appreciation of the key writers and major texts within the Scottish literary tradition.

Lorna Borrowman Smith
Ronald Renton

NOTE ON REFERENCES
Information on the editions of the novels of R.L. Stevenson referred to in this *Scotnote* will be found in the bibliography at the end of this volume

Robert Louis Stevenson: A Brief Life

Robert Louis Stevenson was born in Edinburgh in 1850 and died in Samoa in 1894. Between these two dates and locations, Stevenson travelled an often difficult, complicated life and, although it may be thought that his death was tragically premature, he managed to leave behind a body of fiction that is among the most accomplished prose work in the English language. This accomplishment is registered both in Stevenson's sheer descriptive verve, seen, for instance, in his much commented upon ability to paint dramatic incidents full of movement and tension, and in his presentation of the moral ambiguity of human life. The second of these qualities sits at odds with a somewhat lazy popular perception of Stevenson that grew up in the twentieth century as a "writer of romance" or a "writer of adventure" or even a "children's writer." Much of this false estimation is a result of the fact that cinema has turned to Stevenson's work with a frequency equalled only by the adaptation of the work of Jane Austen and Charles Dickens among British novelists. While the cinematic treatment of Stevenson has not been uniformly bad, it would be true to say that his work has not enjoyed the fine production values that have so often been apparent with regard to Austen and, especially, Dickens.[1] *Treasure Island* and *The Strange Case of Dr Jekyll and Mr Hyde* have lent themselves too easily to the heavily accented swashbuckling gaiety and gothic horror that Hollywood has ever been intent on churning out.

It is certainly true that younger readers can enjoy Stevenson's fiction, but Stevenson is very much an "adult" writer, and we see this when he is writing about childhood experience, which is often noticeably dark in his work. To take one example, *Kidnapped* features an adolescent, David Balfour, who is subject to attempts by his uncle to murder him and sell him into slavery. In the same novel, we find the cabin-boy, Ransome, a pre-teen drunk, who is beaten to death by the alcoholic mate, Mr Shuan. This latter scenario is perhaps something that the uninitiated would expect to find more readily in Irvine Welsh than in Robert Louis Stevenson. Generally, *Kidnapped* also displays a trademark Stevensonian perception, where the adult world is seen as brutal and replete with repressed and exploding selfish motivation. In Stevenson's fiction, "society", including its subset of family, is never as "respectable" as humans might believe it to be or as trustworthy as it claims it ought to be.

With some justification, much speculation has been expended on the effect of Stevenson's own biography on his fiction. A sickly child, Robert spent his early education with private tutors, and, generally, he was somewhat indulged in this situation though he could also, understandably, suffer from loneliness. The Stevensons, who were a famous professional family of engineers, saw Robert embark upon the study of engineering at Edinburgh University when aged seventeen, but after four years he decided to switch to law. He was called to the bar in 1875 though he never finally practised as a lawyer. From the age of twenty-three Stevenson had traumatic, verbally violent confrontations with his devoutly Presbyterian father over his agnosticism. Throughout his life he remained fragile in health and attracted to "alternative" lifestyles, both factors that lay behind his travels in Europe and then much further abroad. His most consistent friend during the first half of his life was his cousin Bob (Robert Alan Mowbray) Stevenson, a similarly rebellious figure so far as his family was concerned. Stevenson visited him in Fontainebleau, France, in 1875, where Bob was involved with a colony of writers and artists. From this point Stevenson developed an increasing love of France and exotic travel and lifestyle. The result of this affection is his first long piece of prose, the travelogue *An Inland Voyage* (1878) documenting his canoe trip around Northern France during 1876. The Stevenson family could sometimes indulgently turn a blind eye to Robert's bohemianism and his dandyism which could appear an affront to douce, Calvinist, Edinburgh in the nineteenth century. (A small example of such behaviour was his Frenchifying of his middle name, which he changed from "Lewis" to "Louis".) They were horrified, however, at his increasing friendship with an older American divorcee, Fanny Osbourne, whom he had met in 1873 and whom he eventually married in 1880. Again, their response to Stevenson was sharply expressed disapproval, but never entire estrangement or complete withdrawal of support. The family remained largely loving toward a son who had changed direction and made awkward choices too many times so far as they were concerned.

Stevenson's *Edinburgh: Picturesque Notes*, published at the same time as *An Inland Voyage*, expressed his impassioned love for Edinburgh and the huge impact the city's geography and history had upon his imagination. His love of Scotland was to stay with him throughout his career, so that, for instance, he wrote his novel of the cultural turmoil following the Jacobite Rebellion of 1745 *Kidnapped* (1886) while living in Bournemouth, and its sequel, *Catriona* (1892), while he was living in the South Seas. In both these novels we find that the seeming romance of the Scottish past masks more sinister realities at work in human society. Alongside *Kidnapped*, Stevenson's most famous novels are *Treasure Island* (1881) and *The Strange Case of Dr Jekyll and Mr Hyde* (1886). The first of these has allowed Stevenson's celebrated reputation as a writer for children, though the real artistry of this novel lies in its astonishingly skilful and sometimes frightening narration of events through the eyes of a young boy, Jim Hawkins. *Jekyll and Hyde,* on the other hand, provides his most telling exploration of the adult mind. What emerges from all of Stevenson's fiction is his brilliance as a psychological writer and an interrogator of cultural mores. Both of these facets are to the fore in his later work, dealing with both his adopted home of Samoa in the South Pacific and his original home of Edinburgh. Increasingly supportive of Samoan rights in the face of British imperial interests in the South Seas, Stevenson justifiably feared deportation from the place in which he had come to live during late 1889. *The Ebb-Tide*, a novel which casts a withering look at white behaviour in the South Seas was published in 1894. Just as powerful as this novel among Stevenson's South Seas fiction is "The Beach of Falesa" (1891), a long short story displaying controlled anger as it surveys inter-racial liaisons in the Pacific islands. The sly painting of the ambiguities of Scottish life and culture that Stevenson had begun in *Kidnapped* was even more darkly developed in *The Master of Ballantrae* (1888) and *Weir of Hermiston* which he had started in 1892 and which was left incomplete on his death in 1894 from a cerebral haemorrhage. With these two novels alongside the best of his South Seas fiction, the evil and pathos of humanity in Stevenson's vision are brilliantly illuminated, and the supposed codes of moral behaviour are scrutinised in ways that are bound to make the reader thoughtfully uncomfortable and to shake any complacency he or she might have about the conceit of civilisation.

Note
1. For a useful select filmography of Stevenson's work, see J.R. Hammond, *A Robert Louis Stevenson Companion* (London, 1984), pp.237-239.

The Strange Case of
Dr Jekyll and Mr Hyde (1886)

The setting is Victorian London. When the eminently respectable Dr Jekyll develops a drug to separate out the good and evil sides of his nature, his malevolent qualities materialise in the form of the depraved and murderous Mr Hyde. Jekyll finds himself increasingly taken over by the personality of Hyde and commits suicide. The strangeness of this story is heightened by its being narrated partly through the testimonies of key participants.

The Culture and Psychology of The Double

When Stevenson's *The Strange Case of Dr Jekyll and Mr Hyde* (1886) was first published one reviewer remarked upon the mismatch between its seeming form as a "shilling work" and the "delicate and restrained skill" of the book.[1] From the beginning, *Jekyll and Hyde* was seen alternately as a work of sensationalism or as a story with subtle and profound things to say about the human condition. On the one hand, a sneering, melodramatic parody of the novel appeared in *Punch* less than a month after its publication, and, on the other, Gerard Manley Hopkins was moved to remark that, "in my judgment the amount of gift and genius which goes into novels in the English literature of this generation is perhaps not so much inferior to what made the Elizabethan drama."[2] Clearly, Stevenson's novel has continued to reverberate widely in popular cultural consciousness and in the psychological interests of a modern, post-Freudian age. *Jekyll and Hyde* is an extraordinarily prescient work, preceding the infamous "Jack the Ripper" murders in London's East End by two years. The roots of much of the theorising over possible identities for the killer is prompted by the idea in *Jekyll and Hyde* of a character who is a pillar of society harbouring horrible sociopathic tendencies. Stevenson also seems to be pointing towards the then unknown work of Sigmund Freud and the development of psychoanalysis with its key concepts of the superego (socially conditioned self-image and self-restraint) and the id (primitive, volatile instinct). As a household coinage for the "split personality", *Jekyll and Hyde* has populated numerous comedy sketches, horror films, and literary re-explanations during the twentieth century, becoming an iconic figure, or a new "everyman", for a supposed age of cultural, social and spiritual fragmentation. To take only two examples from literature, the re-using of *Jekyll and Hyde* can be found in Duncan McLean's *Bunker Man* (1995) as a critique of barely repressed violence in working-class Scottish life, and in Emma Tennant's *Two Women of London: The Strange Case of Ms Jekyll and Mrs Hyde* (1989) where the scenario is given a gender twist.

The idea of the doubled personality in *Jekyll and Hyde* is not, of course, entirely the innovation of Stevenson. Precedents are to be found for the interest in the alternative or split self in English literature in such diverse texts as William Shakespeare's *The Comedy of Errors* (first acted in 1592 or 1594) and Christopher Marlowe's *Doctor Faustus* (1604). Most directly pertinent to Stevenson, however, are those texts featuring doppelgängers found in nineteenth century Romanticism. For instance, Mary Shelley's *Frankenstein* (1818); the supernatural tales of Edgar Allan Poe, who is sometimes claimed to have led a very sordid, hidden life; and Nathaniel Hawthorne's *The Scarlet Letter* (1850) are works that exemplify the interest in transgressing or escaping the normal mores of society via secret selves.

In the Scottish context the notion of insidiously ambidextrous character is to be found in a tradition whose most spectacular examples are Robert Burns's poem, "Holy Willie's Prayer" (written in 1785 but not routinely published in the most complete versions of Burns's work until the 1890s), and James Hogg's *Private Memoirs and Confessions of a Justified Sinner* (1824). The origins of this Scottish depiction lie in an aristocratic, high Tory attitude of the late seventeenth and early eighteenth centuries which satirised the fanatical, fun-suppressing nature of a Puritanical Whig or Calvinist Scottish culture. Pro-Jacobite poets in Scots, such as Allan Ramsay (1684-1758) in his "Elegy on John Cowper, Kirk-Treasurer's Man", (1718) castigate the dour, but secretly sinning Calvinist personality; and later Burns, himself from an essentially Presbyterian background, raises this depiction to a new height of psychological frenzy in the figure of Willie. In turn another Presbyterian, James Hogg, develops such a portrait to the extent of portraying mental disintegration in one of the great psychological novels of the Romantic period. In spite of their odiousness both Burns's Willie and Hogg's Robert Wringhim encompass the Romantic interest in peculiar or exotic personalities. If these two depictions do not exactly give rise to

sympathetic portraits, they establish a type less easily to be
laughed at or simply dismissed than those one-dimensional
Calvinist stereotypes wielded by earlier writers such as Ramsay.
This is all the more the case with Hogg who draws upon a deep
well of folk-tradition pertaining to the doppelgänger. The
protean or shape-changing propensities of demons and the Devil
in western culture can be traced at least as far back as Christ's
driving out into a herd of swine an evil spirit in the Gospel of
Mark. This demon's answer to Christ's interrogation of its
identity is to indicate its multiplicity in the response, "My name
is legion for we are many" (*Mark* 5:9).

The dualistic nature of humanity is also a prominent idea in
Christian theology. An interesting phenomenon with regard to
Jekyll and Hyde is the contemporary use made of the tale in the
pulpit. For instance, one theological writer expressed the view
that Stevenson's novel was "an allegory based on the two-fold
nature of man, a truth I find taught to us by the Apostle Paul in
Romans vii, 'I find then a law that, when I would do good, evil is
present with me'."[3] Arguably, this supposed nature comes to the
cultural fore in the claustrophobic atmosphere of Victorian
society. The literary example of the life and work of Oscar Wilde
stands out here. Among other works, Wilde published his *The
Picture of Dorian Gray* (1891) a tale of divided self, and it has
been suggested that just as Wilde's novel has to do with his
suppressed and dissociated identity as a homosexual, so too
Jekyll and Hyde has a sexual subtext. The Victorian period with
its intense social certainties amidst a rapidly changing world of
belief was a watershed of the modern age and interests in
rationality, religious doubt and science all feature in *Jekyll and
Hyde*. A nicely and probably unintentionally ironic remark by
J.A. Symonds, casts Stevenson himself almost as a Jekyll and
Hyde figure. Even as he wrote to Stevenson expressing large
admiration for the novel, Symonds expressed the doubt that, "It
makes me wonder whether a man has the right so to scrutinize
'the abysmal deeps of personality'."[4] This remark captures
something of the intensity of Stevenson's *Jekyll and Hyde* that
marks it out very much as a work of the modern age as it
explores urges in human behaviour that everyday society finds
difficult to acknowledge.

Through the twentieth century, repression leading to
disordered duality as a theme features very strongly in Scottish
writing and includes, to list only a few of the most famous
examples, James Bridie's depiction of Robert Knox in *The*

Anatomist (1930), Robin Jenkins's Duror in *The Cone Gatherers* (1955) and Muriel Spark's eponymous character in *The Prime of Miss Jean Brodie* (1961). In all of these works we find individuals who believe themselves to be above the normal moral code in the interests of pursuing knowledge or "the truth." This powerful canon of Scottish texts is often read in the light of the inspiring power of *Jekyll and Hyde*.

Characterisation: Social Roles
On the surface the characterisation in *Jekyll and Hyde* is deliberately sketchy, in keeping with its theme of the hidden personality. The central character and others are largely defined by the social roles in which they are cloaked, and to some extent, cosseted. The main protagonists represent professional certainty and, particularly, male confidence and complicity. It is interesting that at one point Hyde is heard "weeping like a woman or a lost soul" (p.44). The idea of repressed femininity and the primacy of the male are oblique factors throughout the novel. The text features shared male secrets and companionship, seen, for instance, as Mr Utterson moves only very slowly to act upon his suspicions about Jekyll who has been his youthful friend. The man of medicine, Dr Lanyon; Jekyll's butler, Poole; the member of parliament, Sir Danvers Carew and Utterson are all representatives of a patriarchal class system whose lives are shaken by Jekyll's rebellious transformation. The novel hints that Jekyll's dualistic nature is part of a wider condition. Repression by social orderliness for which the city of London is emblematic is conjoined with a darker side of human behaviour that also exists as a kind of underbelly to the metropolis. Not much is made of this explicitly in *Jekyll and Hyde*. The conditions of the British capital were well known in the 1880s to contain sinks of human misery and corruption, something that Charles Dickens in his fiction had helped to register indelibly in the minds of the intelligentsia from the mid-point of the nineteenth century. Stevenson's London is a claustrophobic, physically foggy environment where the underside is subtly, if opaquely, sketched. For instance, Utterson's "distant kinsman" (p.6), Richard Enfield, is someone who beneath his façade of being "the well-known man about town" (p.6) is rather more mysterious than this description would suggest. Like Jekyll, Enfield is a character whose personality and actions are never entirely spelled out. He describes his initial meeting with Hyde as occurring as he, Enfield, returns "from some place at the end

of the world, about three o'clock of a black winter morning" (p.7).
What Enfield's activities have been on that night we never learn,
but his own vagueness as to where he has been might point us
toward the suspicion of some form of debauchery he is either
unwilling or unable to remember. Enfield too, then, is a perhaps a
kind of "Jekyll and Hyde" character.

Jekyll the Scientist
Henry Jekyll represents the familiar type of the scientist pushing
the bounds of human experimentalism, and in this scenario, he
stands in a line that can be taken back through Shelley's Dr
Frankenstein to Marlowe's Dr Faust. Dr Jekyll is scientifically
interested in the truth of the identity or personality and his self-
experimentation convinces him that human beings contain
"multifarious, incongruous and independent" (p.56) natures
within the one organism. His conclusion, then, is that the notion
of coherence or harmony in human identity is inaccurate, so he is
implicitly challenging the idea of human order upon which civil
society is largely based. Particularly, he sees humanity made of
selfish as well as sociable urges, of evil as well as good. In
theological terms, Jekyll arguably partakes of the historical
heresy of Manichaeism, believing that good and evil are conjoined
in a spiritual state of equilibrium. He believes that he is "radically
both" (p.56), equally just and unjust in his nature and wishes to
separate these two personalities out so that neither is hampered
by the other. Such a solution to the contradiction in human urges,
which allows both to have free rein at different moments, is
Jekyll's perhaps initially attractive solution, but this is morally
and socially simplistic. We see this in the results where Hyde, as
embodiment of bad desires, grows increasingly strong and
murderous in tandem with the decreasing power of the "good"
Jekyll. Jekyll seeks neat separation of elements in the face of the
messiness of the human personality, but succeeds only in
accentuating the battle between the contradictory impetuses of
human nature.
    Jekyll's language indicates contempt toward the human body
as he talks of his chemical discoveries that allow him "to shake
and to pluck back that fleshly vestment, even as a wind might toss
the curtains of a pavilion" (p.56). Jekyll uses a particularly
impious turn of phrase as he talks of the physical body as "that
immaterial tabernacle" (p.57). Jekyll is here close to being the
clinical, atheistic scientist deliberately dissenting from the view
held in Christianity (as well as in all the other major religions of

the world) that both the body and the more mysterious spirit (or soul) demand respect as the unified work of a divine creator. One might read Jekyll's dissolution and death in orthodox fashion as the punishment for arrogant impiety. He is the scientist as perfectionist who will not accept the irregularities or the lack of cogency in human existence that Christianity and other religions suggest is entailed in the mystery of earthly identity.

As he worries over the relation of his friend, Jekyll, to Hyde at the beginning of the novel, the lawyer Utterson alludes in a very unspecific manner to previous irregularities in Jekyll's life.

> "Poor Harry Jekyll," he thought, "my mind misgives me he is in deep waters! He was wild when he was young; a long while ago to be sure; but in the law of God there is no statute of limitations. Ay, it must be that; the ghost of some old sin, the cancer of some concealed disgrace: punishment coming, *pede claudo* [limping along behind], years after memory has forgotten and self-love condoned the fault." (p.17)

Utterson sees Jekyll as perhaps suffering guilt over some unpunished wrong he has perpetrated long ago. The truth though is that Jekyll until recently has dampened down, rather than corrected, his previous character. Jekyll was "wild" when he was young and it is this wildness that has returned in the shape of Hyde. It is not good conscience that is haunting Jekyll but a suppressed evil urge. Utterson's reading of the situation, then, is completely the wrong way round, and beneath his veneer of respectability as a man of the law who encompasses also the workings of God in his calculations, we might notice also his complacency. He is essentially unconcerned that his friend should have "some concealed disgrace" and he is discreet, or euphemistic, even in his internal musings so that he is not specific with regard to the nature of Jekyll's former "wildness." This opens up the possibility of reading Jekyll's malaise as lying in the fact that his place in society and his fellows of the same class have hitherto failed to check his excesses so long as they stay hidden. Jekyll's most spectacular excesses, then, in his self-experimentation are the product of a man whom no one has questioned in the past, as ought to have been done. Jekyll himself suggests that so long as he is discreet in his "pleasures", he can carry on as a respectable professional man:

> [T]he worst of my faults was a certain impatient
> gaiety of disposition, such as has made the
> happiness of many, but such as I found it hard to
> reconcile with my imperious desire to carry my head
> high, and wear a more than commonly grave
> countenance before the public. Hence it came about
> that I concealed my pleasures; and that when I
> reached years of reflection, and began to look round
> me and take stock of my progress and position in the
> world, I stood already committed to a profound
> duplicity of life. (p.55)

Even here, in Jekyll's account left as written "confession", we
notice that the scientist is circumspect about the precise nature of
his "pleasures." Reserve is the watchword to the end for the sake
of preserving respectable social appearance among this class of
male professional.

Utterson, a Man to be Trusted
The lawyer Utterson is concerned primarily that his friend Jekyll
should regain his equanimity of mind: " 'Jekyll,' said Utterson, 'you
know me: I am a man to be trusted. Make a clean breast of this in
confidence; and I make no doubt I can get you out of it'" (p.20). What
Utterson means when he says that he is "a man to be trusted" is
that he is a man who can keep a secret, and so, as readers, we ought
to see him as part of the fabric of wrong-headed, dark concealment
that is so pervasive in the novel. According to his own lights
Utterson is a man who tries to help a friend, a man who cares about
morality and who tries to deal actively with the situation of Jekyll
as it unfolds. However, all of these things are done very
circumspectly so as to avoid social scandal. For instance, Utterson
more or less hides evidence from the police in the case of the Carew
murder by taking into his own possession the letter shown to him
by Jekyll and ostensibly written by Hyde implicitly confessing to
the crime. Such suppression at this point is not even to protect the
fact that his friend in his alter ego is the murderer, but to protect
the reputation of Jekyll, whom Lanyon believes perhaps merely to
have forged the letter to help the homicidal Hyde. Thus we see
Utterson complicit in keeping up the outward appearance of the
respectable society of which he and Jekyll are a part. The name
"Hyde", of course, points with heavy irony toward the notion of
concealment (the game of "Hide and Seek"), and Utterson too is
party to hiding the truth, at times in all too frivolous a fashion. The
lawyer's name is presumably derived from the term "utter

barrister" denoting a rank of lawyer who is not a king's or queen's counsel. What point might Stevenson be making in adopting such a naming strategy, where characters are hidebound (or hydebound) by their professional or other surface appellations? It adds to the thematic texture of the novel where outward appearance is important to the characters of a society that does not wish to acknowledge what is going on under the surface or behind closed doors. Another example of the deliberately facile naming process is to be found in the "man about town", Enfield, who, in accordance with such an epithet is ironically named after a London borough. He too, as we have seen, is keen to maintain a seemingly straightforward persona, while actually harbouring more opaque behaviour. Irony can be read also in Utterson's name since he fails for a long time – even to himself despite his obviously growing awareness – to *utter on* (utterance being his main professional tool as a lawyer) his knowledge of Jekyll's secret.

Utterson: A Trapped Humanity
Utterson himself is a divided character. He is habitually unsmiling and reserved, although when drinking wine in the company of friends, "something eminently human beaconed from his eye; something indeed which never found its way into his talk" (p.5). In this metaphor, humanity is trapped within Utterson who drinks gin alone and who, "though he enjoyed the theatre, had not crossed the doors of one for twenty years" (p.5). He is prone not to judge and is emotionally detached from the iniquity he encounters in his everyday professional life. We are told that he says of himself, "'I incline to Cain's heresy,' he used to say quaintly: 'I let my brother go to the devil in his own way'" (p.5). What he means in the latter phrase is that he will not interfere with the conduct of others. The biblical reference is to Cain who murdered his brother, Abel, to take his possessions and out of jealousy that the latter's offering had been more acceptable to God. This works, of course, as a forward-glancing allusion to the bad "brother", Hyde, who "destroys" the socially acceptable, good "brother" Jekyll. Without moral intervention Utterson allows others to condemn themselves from their own mouths with whatever lies and iniquity they choose. Here we find not stereotypically stern Victorian patriarchal moralising in Utterson's character, but an untroubled, accepting approach to the reality of individual wickedness of the human world. Utterson, then, is "undemonstrative" (p.5) either in expressing any joy or any condemnation in the face of human nature. As the story progresses though, Utterson becomes more

fearful in the face of the depravity that he encounters in Jekyll/
Hyde. His complacency, like that of Lanyon, is shaken. He is forced
to become more active in response to Jekyll's dissolution. He
initially chooses to believe that Jekyll has disappeared as a result
of having been murdered by Hyde. As, however, he prevents the
servants from entering Jekyll's locked room and as he entreats the
silence of Jekyll's butler, Poole, Utterson is more concerned to hush
up rather than deal with the evil he increasingly suspects to be the
responsibility of his friend. The stock eighteenth century device of
providing the lawyer with a caricatured name is used very
ironically here. Utterson, in fact, is desperate not to articulate, at
least publicly, the growing evidence of Jekyll's wrongdoing.

Dr Lanyon's Despair
As well as the death of Carew and Jekyll himself, the novel also
features the fatal illness of Dr Lanyon. Lanyon receives a visit
from Hyde after Jekyll has indicated to him that his emissary will
furnish him with an explanation of the scientist's mysterious
behaviour. Typical of the irony with which the novel is replete, he
asks Hyde, "'Are you come from Dr Jekyll?'" (p.51). Lanyon
describes his experience of Hyde:

> He was small, as I have said; I was struck besides
> with the shocking expression of his face, with his
> remarkable combination of great muscular activity
> and great apparent debility of constitution, and –
> last but not least – with the odd, subjective
> disturbance caused by his neighbourhood. This bore
> some resemblance to incipient rigor and was
> accompanied by a marked sinking of the pulse. At
> the time, I set it down to some idiosyncratic,
> personal distaste, and merely wondered at the
> acuteness of the symptoms; but I have since had
> reason to believe the cause to lie much deeper in the
> nature of man, and to turn on some nobler hinge
> than the principle of hatred. (p.51)

This is one of the most important passages in the novel. The doctor's
metabolism slows down; he is transformed, though to a much lesser
extent than Jekyll. It is as though the doctor knows that he is in the
presence of the deathly, and his response is at once sympathetic (in a
neutral sense) and also judgemental in that he can intuit the
badness of humanity. Why does Lanyon succumb to an unnamed
illness and die so soon after this experience? The first clue to this

question lies, perhaps, in the scientific precision with which he describes his encounter with Hyde. In his account we have the implicit indication of a fear that became increasingly widespread in the Victorian age, most especially after the epoch-moulding proposition by Charles Darwin of the theory of evolution. By the end of the nineteenth century, there was a prominent strand of thought in western culture that feared that science was proving humanity to be merely part of the material animal and chemical reality of nature, rather than God's chosen creature whose spiritual mission was the pursuit of virtue. Jekyll's scientific quest for his evil side as he degenerates or evolves backwards into Hyde seriously undermines the optimistic Victorian idea of the progress of moral enlightenment. Lanyon, the man of science, seems to lapse into a despair which precipitates his death in the face of the knowledge that evil can be distilled more easily than the good side of human nature. The most logical reading of his death is that he is unable to continue living in a universe where the primacy of good can no longer taken for granted. In this he is an embryonic precursor of a later type in twentieth century fiction: the character who endures angst in a Godless universe. Another question remains, however. Is Lanyon's capitulation in the face of his knowledge the only possible response? On the one hand, we might have sympathy with his surrender, given the darkness and horror of what he has seen. On the other, we might argue that he exemplifies the ultimate shallowness of a certain cosy Victorian Christian and social outlook that fails to see that evil is always with us and constantly finds new *transformations* (such shape-changing of the Devil being his *modus operandi*) with which to confront humanity.

Jekyll and the Justified Sinner

In the fate of Jekyll, we see humanity hoist with its own scientific petard. As he frames his memoir we see that out of seeming experimental precision has come profound uncertainty for the scientist:

> Should the throes of change take me in the act of writing it, Hyde will tear it in pieces; but if some time shall have elapsed after I have laid it by, his wonderful selfishness and circumscription to the moment will probably save it once again from the action of his ape-like spite. And indeed the doom that is closing on us both, has already changed and crushed him. Half an hour from now, when I shall

> again and for ever reindue that hated personality, I
> know how I shall sit shuddering and weeping in my
> chair, or continue, with the most strained and
> fearstruck ecstasy of listening, to pace up and down
> this room (my last earthly refuge) and give ear to
> every sound of menace. Will Hyde die upon the
> scaffold? or will he find the courage to release himself
> at the last moment? God knows; I am careless; this is
> my true hour of death, and what is to follow concerns
> another than myself. Here, then, as I lay down the
> pen, and proceed to seal up my confession, I bring the
> life of that unhappy Henry Jekyll to an end. (p.70)

We have here an echo of the fate of James Hogg's Robert Wringhim
in *The Private Memoirs and Confessions of a Justified Sinner* as he
shelters at the end of his life in a cottage fearfully listening for the
demons without, whom he believes to be pursuing him. Like
Wringhim, Jekyll has also resorted to the ancient Christian mode of
confessional writing, setting down his wrongs for the scrutiny of
others. Again, like Wringhim, Jekyll is actually in hiding from his
own malevolent nature to which he has given free rein. Is *Jekyll
and Hyde*, then, to be read as a conventional morality tale, where
over-reaching   arrogance   is   rewarded   with   downfall   and
punishment, and the lesson for the reader is that ultimately human
beings are never as in control of their destinies as they think they
are? Such a reading would be consonant with the attack on
Calvinism (with its doctrines of election and predestination) in
Hogg's *Confessions of a Justified Sinner*. Indeed, we might see
Stevenson's work as a transposition of Hogg's method to encompass
a more general warning against the optimistic certainty inherent in
some forms of modern scientific experimentation and enquiry.

The Narrative: Oppositions
Jekyll and Hyde is a novel that draws on large, perhaps primeval,
oppositions such as light and darkness, adult and child or male and
female for its resonances and is a quite deliberately mysterious
work as part of its psychological methodology. It provides scenarios
where we are not given enough information to explicate these
entirely. We never know precisely why Hyde should trample upon
the girl after they seem to run into one another accidentally. The
most we can make of the incident is that Hyde is monstrously
selfish, as the expected adult solicitousness is absent in Hyde's
behaviour. He transgresses the supposed normal rules of society in
his treatment of the child. We have another very primal narrative

opposition as the murder of Sir Danvers Carew is witnessed by the maid from the window. She is at peace with the world and is enjoying a romantic reverie in the light of the full moon:

> And as she so sat she became aware of an aged and beautiful gentleman with white hair drawing near along the lane ... the moon shone on his face as he spoke, and the girl was pleased to watch it, it seemed to breath such an innocent and old-world kindness of disposition ... (p.21)

The maid's story is seemingly straightforward. The stock-character of a romantic young girl sees "innocence" and "kindness" abroad in the world, which shortly she is horrified to see being brutally murdered as Hyde appears on the scene. We have, it would appear, the opposition of simple good versus motiveless evil as Hyde clubs and stamps Carew to death. We should, however, be on the alert from the moment that the maid projects her idea of virtue upon Carew. It is her one-dimensional perception that is in play here rather than an objective view of what is really going on in the street. She sees Carew solicit conversation with Hyde, "as if he were only inquiring his way" (p.21). This, however, immediately throws up a mystery: what is Carew trying to find out? Where is he going? Some critics have suggested that Carew is in search of a homosexual encounter and that this is what provokes the rage of Hyde. Arguably, there is a hint of this nature in Carew's "very pretty manner of politeness" (p.21), though it might be that such a reading also makes up a story, just as the maid has done, through the lens of a very modern mindset. The idea of sexuality being bound up in the episode would, however, make some sense in that this would represent another repressed and conventionally frowned upon element in society. Carew would have to go covertly in search of such an experience at night and to a seeming stranger. The pattern, then, would be that the manically liberated Hyde destroys a suppressed element similar to himself so that there is a downward spiral of suppressed behaviour. Society in suppressing certain urges lets these loose, ultimately, in the most dangerous back-street fashion. Carew, like many others in the novel, is a character of whom we do not have enough knowledge from which to draw any conclusion. Instead what we have, potentially, are two sets of perceptions. We have the maid's conventional view of Carew's essentially uncomplicated virtue and the aware reader's, whose perception of a more complex Carew will be activated, but never entirely satisfied.

On this reading the reader actively collaborates with the novel in bringing to it the idea of surface and hidden reality, or duplicitous reality, that is such a repeated motif throughout the novel.

The Narrative: Unsettling Techniques
We have mentioned already the carapace of respectability attached to characters such as Jekyll, most obviously, and Enfield, whose hidden life is registered much more obliquely. We have mentioned also the implicit dissent in *Jekyll and Hyde* from the notion that the city is a rational, functional machine of business and industry; instead London in the novel harbours less easily managed human urges and neuroses. The tendency of writers to see the urban setting and society, generally, as not simply a practical formation but as perhaps even encouraging a kind of madness had been developing since at least the late eighteenth century. The *strangeness* of the city as a place of alienated individuals and lost souls becomes particularly apparent, however, in the Victorian era with such texts as James (B.V.) Thomson's *City of Dreadful Night* (1874), where a central character feels all the more oppressively alone amidst the pretensions of the urban setting to make sense. This line of city-weary literature stretches from the "crisis of faith" of the late nineteenth century down to the Modernist period of the early twentieth century, where particularly intense disquiet is registered in the likes of T.S. Eliot's "The Love Song of J. Alfred Prufrock" (1917).

Jekyll and Hyde contributes to the canon of literature in which the city is a fearful, lonely and unsettling place. Overwhelmingly, this effect is not achieved by direct description of the city but by the management of space, both the physical space of the setting in the novel and its narrative space. The various units of the novel are deliberately uneven in size making up a ragged whole. They are perhaps not best described as chapters, and editions of the novel usually dispense with numbered ordering. The first section is entitled, "Story of the Door". Immediately, then, we are confronted with a "close-up" feature in the urban setting, which before long, we realise, leads into a mysterious and sinister space, but which for the moment denies access to the reader. The vicinity of the door is a busy and primitive place:

> The door, which was equipped with neither bell nor knocker, was blistered and distained. Tramps slouched into the recess and struck matches on the panels; children kept shop upon the steps; the schoolboy had

tried his knife on the mouldings; and for close on a generation no one had appeared to drive away these random visitors or to repair their ravages. (p.6)

This back-street location, then, is a forgotten place of rather feral, largely male activity. Although a functional point of access, an opening, it seems to have become almost a darkly totemic space in its own right.

This is the door into which Hyde goes to retrieve the cheque to make reparation to the trampled girl's family when Enfield and others corner him. Enfield, however, is unwilling to delve too deeply into the house. He indicates that he does not wish to open up any embarrassing situation and says of the house and Hyde's occupancy of it, "the more it looks like Queer Street, the less I ask" (p.9). Enfield clearly believes that Hyde is connected with some probably respectable family fallen into slightly embarrassed financial and socially scandalous times. The cliché of "Queer Street" in the scenario of this novel, however, carries greater purchase since it points again to the idea of transformation. With this house and with the setting of much of the novel we are in a strange area of unmapped, or altered geography. Later we learn that the door is merely the back of a more respectable address and façade, and this contributes to the figure and theme of reversibility in the novel. Even the street here has a Jekyll and Hyde quality to it, suggesting, perhaps the "strange case" is not quite so strange or unique to Dr Jekyll as at first might be thought. The possession of a dark underside, or an alternative passageway, pertains more widely in society than simply to this one man.

The constricted space within which the action is conducted is again seen in Hyde's secretive midnight visit to Dr Lanyon's house, and in the maid's witnessing of the murder of Carew through a window. Throughout the novel we are given the impression of tightly constrained space, with the ultimate claustrophobic reality being that of Jekyll confined to his laboratory as he can no longer control his transformations. The fragmentary and highly subjective narrative in which *Jekyll and Hyde* is transmitted to the reader contributes to this texture of hidden and secretive space and complements the idea of social reality as something less complete than it is usually taken to be. We might suggest that the novel is something of a pre-Modernist work in form as well as theme, as it eschews any one absolutely authoritative narrator and is made up of a series of uneven narratorial documents. A particularly unsettling technique adopted by Stevenson is the sequencing of the narrative elements. We begin with an omniscient, third person narrator, move to the terrified written account left by Dr Lanyon and end with the despair of Jekyll's own written confession. Added to this, we have a peppering of confusing narrative documents such as Hyde's letter and Jekyll's will.

A Plea for Honesty?
At the end of Jekyll's confession, no narrative voice returns to "tidy" things up. We are left instead with a somewhat numb conclusion rather than the implicitly optimistic restoration of narrative order. We are left with the words of a hopeless, dying man. As with the question of where the door leads to, then, we have a slow process of interior and increasingly depressing revelation. Beneath the general effect of omniscient narration that comprises the first eight sections of the novel, we also have the story of Enfield in the opening section, with its oblique undertow of personal mystery and obfuscation. This is the first component in the Babushka doll effect of *Jekyll and Hyde* where we are taken deeper and deeper inside the situation through a series of individually reported stories. Amidst the fragmentation, dark motivation and despair of the novel there is, however, an implicit appeal to personal and social openness. Insofar as *Jekyll and Hyde* carries a practical message it perhaps consists in this plea for greater human honesty.

Notes
1. Andrew Lang, An Unsigned Review, 'Saturday Review' reprinted in Paul Maixner (ed.), *Robert Louis Stevenson: The Critical Heritage* (London, 1981), pp.199-202. Hereafter RLSCH.
2. For the parody in *Punch* of 6 February 1886 see *RLSCH* pp.208-210; and for Hopkins's remarks in a letter of 28 October 1886 to Robert Bridges see *RLSCH* pp.228-230.
3. See the unsigned review from *'The Rock'* (2 April 1886, 3), a journal of the Unified Church of England and Ireland, reprinted in *RLSCH*, pp.224-227.
4. For J.A. Symonds' letter of 3 March 1886 to RLS see *RLSCH*, pp.210-211.

The Master of Ballantrae (1889)

This novel, set in Scotland and Canada in the aftermath of the Jacobite defeat at Culloden, revisits Stevenson's previous interest in human depravity. It traces the tragic conflict of the two Duries, the pernicious James and his younger brother Henry, over the family estates of Durrisdeer and Ballantrae. The bleak, wintry account is coloured by the personality of the narrator Mackellar, the family's long-serving steward.

Stevenson and Historical Romance

Reviewing *The Master of Ballantrae* when it first appeared, W.E. Henley wrote that it is:

> [...] one of the gloomiest, or rather the grimiest of stories. There is not a noble nor a loveable character in the book: the narrator is a poltroon; the hero is a devil in human shape, while his arch-enemy sinks into a vindictive dullard; the one woman in the story is morbidly enamoured of her husband's brother; the chief scene is a scene of fratricidal strife; the supernumeraries are a choice assortment of smugglers, pirates, murderers and mutineers; than the plot there is nothing uglier in Balzac.[1]

Henley rounds off this dark litany with the comment that "the whole thing is a triumph of imagination and literary art."[2] This contemporary admiration of Stevenson's craftsmanship sits somewhat at odds with his subsequent long fall from critical favour. Broadly, this unfashionable turn that his work took was not so much to do with any change of opinion on Stevenson's technical, or stylistic capability (over the past one hundred and twenty years he has consistently been seen as one of the great prose writers in the English – as well as the Scots – language), but has to do with the impression that Stevenson indulged too often in the romance and adventure mode. In one mood, Stevenson was genuinely a writer of historical romance as we see in *Kidnapped* (1886). This Jacobite adventure story, where Stevenson has great personal fun replaying the scenario of Walter Scott's *Waverley* (1814), and also *Treasure Island* (1883) have been longstanding children's favourites and were devoured in their own

day by a public keen for period entertainment in the case of the
one and the foreign setting of sunny climes overseas in the other.
Much as today's television audience consumes costume drama,
Victorian readers had an exotic tooth and this allowed Stevenson
a degree of much-needed commercial viability. Part of the
brilliance of his prose lies in its readability to which generation
after generation of readers have attested. Ultimately though, the
"popular" reputation that Stevenson attained here has tended to
overshadow his wider achievement.

Even as *The Master of Ballantrae* is a historical novel dealing
with the turbulent cultural events of eighteenth century Scotland,
it also displays its late nineteenth century "modernity." The
jaundiced cast of characters described by Henley shows Stevenson
continuing, in this genre, his exploration of a preponderantly dark
and shadowy human nature such as he had dealt with in *Jekyll
and Hyde*. Unlike Walter Scott's historical fiction, *The Master of
Ballantrae* offers no easily identifiable "good" or "noble" characters.
We might also notice that the Jacobite rebellion, while relevant to
the plot, is not important to the action of the novel, occurring
essentially "off-stage." *The Master of Ballantrae* gestures towards
certain presuppositions about its historical genre. Ultimately,
however, it actually raises questions about the value of the concept
of "history" for understanding human life (something which makes
it a rather strange "historical" novel). Perhaps Stevenson is
consciously straying into the territory of Scottish Jacobitism, the
subject-matter with which Walter Scott is often held to have
invented the historical novel in *Waverley*, precisely in order to
raise awkward questions about the understanding of history.
Another rather deceptive device is the sub-genre tag, "A Winter's
Tale", which Stevenson provides for *The Master of Ballantrae*. This
description might seem to promise the idea of entertainment,
especially for dark evenings – a ghost story perhaps. But it does
more than this; it delineates the mood of human pessimism that
informs the book and makes it suggest that the darker side of
humanity is most often triumphant in real life.

Playing with Types of Story
As with *Jekyll and Hyde*, *The Master of Ballantrae* indulges in
narratorial framing, so that it includes a preface written by an
"editor" who has obtained the story from Mr Johnstone Thomson,
W.S. (writer to the signet, or a lawyer). His legal friend promises
this editor who has been "exiled" from his native Edinburgh but
who has briefly returned "a mystery":

"Yes," said his friend, "a mystery. It may prove to be nothing, and it may prove to be a great deal. But in the meanwhile it is truly mysterious, no eye having looked on it for near a hundred years; it is highly genteel, for it treats of a titled family; and it ought to be melodramatic, for (according to the superscription) it is concerned with death." (p.6)

The lawyer has recently come into papers in the hand of Ephraim Mackellar, estate steward to the now ruined family of Durie of Durrisdeer and Ballantrae in the South West of Scotland in the mid eighteenth century. Thomson prompts the editor:

"Here," said Mr. Thomson, "is a novel ready to your hand: all you have to do is to work up the scenery, develop the characters, and improve the style."
"My dear fellow," said I, "they are just the three things that I would rather die than set my hand to. It shall be published as it stands."
"But it's so bald," objected Mr. Thomson.
"I believe there is nothing so noble as baldness," replied I, "and I am sure there is nothing so interesting. I would have all literature bald [...]" (p.8)

We might notice here a certain playfulness on the part of Stevenson. Clearly, he has in mind his own situation as cultural émigré and is to be identified with the figure of "the editor." Stevenson, a dilettante in the eyes of his family for having forsaken a career in the law and for turning instead to the life of the imagination, has his editor draw upon a legal archive for the source of the story we are about to be told. There is a nice joke in the editor's culling of a "mystery" and "a melodrama", as Thomson describes it, from papers that are in legal custody. We come to learn that the mystery of the novel revolves around the ostentatious, adventuring and evil behaviour of James, the eldest son of the Durrisdeer family. Related to this puzzle is the hint that we have from the conversations between the lawyer and the editor at the outset that the Durrisdeer family-line has died out early in the nineteenth century. What we are to anticipate, then, is a tale of dynastic downfall and we are teased with ideas of the "melodrama" and the "baldness" of the story which we are to be told. Taken together, these two qualities suggest that an over-sensationalised, and somewhat theatrical account will ensue which is high in emotional nuance but low in fleshed out detail (such as fuller characterisation, as Thomson suggests adding). If the editor were to make the story much fuller, the lawyer says, it would easily become a novel. We have here an interesting comment on the art of the creative writer which implies that the novelist is someone who applies his imagination to offer rounded perspectives upon human life. It might be suggested that this view of the writer of fiction reached its apotheosis during the nineteenth century in the fiction of Charles Dickens and of George Eliot where seemingly random quirks of fate dictate the lives of protagonists who gradually learn that there are more forces at work in the paths of their lives, the working out of which helps them (and the reader) to come to a fuller understanding of human psychology. *The Master of Ballantrae* represents something of a reaction against this type of fiction in that even after the events of its plot have all been worked out, the motivations of the chief characters remain difficult and entangled until the end. This is not to say that it lacks potential insight into human psychological motivation.

The Family-Saga of the Duries of Durrisdeer and Ballantrae

The papers that come into the editor's hands make for a family saga, and these are largely in the hand of Ephraim Mackellar who, if not exactly an unreliable narrator, is certainly not an impartial one. Mackellar himself indicates this fact in a line replete with dramatic irony near the opening of the novel proper: "It so befell that I was intimately mingled with the last years and history of the house [of Durrisdeer]" (p.9).

Mackellar is "intimately mingled" in his narration of the strife of his master's house in the aftermath of the Jacobite rebellion of 1745 in that his sympathies are very much engaged with the family. Most explicitly, he is sympathetic to Henry Durrisdeer, the much put upon younger brother who tries hard to manage his family's affairs after the self-ousting of the first heir, Henry's brother James, who has followed his own dearest desire in rallying to the standard of Charles Edward Stuart when this risky role properly belonged to the cadet brother. As was the case with a number of real historical families during the Jacobite uprising, the Durrisdeer family is supposedly operating the expedient of hedging bets: one brother rebelling, most safely the younger sibling, and one remaining loyal to the dynastic status quo. Family expedience is immediately undercut, however, by James who demands that a coin is tossed to decide which brother goes off in support of the rebellion. James wins and further thoughtless dereliction is added to the situation in that the boys' father, Lord Durisdeer, makes no very great effort to prevent this action once the "decision" has been reached.

Mackellar never offers any criticism of Lord Durrisdeer even though he is plainly and frequently indulgent towards James, his favourite son. We learn that the neighbourhood around the family estate has become unruly and that smugglers operate fairly freely when we might expect Lord Durrisdeer to enforce law and order as his status would have entitled him to do. As we gather later, James is in league with smugglers who rescue him after he has seemingly been killed in a sword fight with his brother. The implication, then, is that his son's trafficking with these outlaws compromises Lord Durrisdeer in his local role as community, as well as family, leader. We also have the shadowy but important implication of financial mismanagement in that the future fiscal health of the family estate depends upon the marriage of the house of Durrisdeer to his lordship's ward, Alison, so that her fortune may allow solvency. How the family has found itself in difficulty is never entirely clear. It may be that Lord Durisdeer, who is close at certain points in the novel to being reclusive, is a weak, impractical man not only in indulging his eldest son, but also in his management of business affairs. Nonetheless, Mackellar remains assiduously loyal to his lordship in never voicing, nor even pointedly hinting at, this scenario. More strangely, we must add to Mackellar's loyalty both to Henry and Lord Durrisdeer, his obvious feelings that James, in spite of his odious behaviour in returning to persecute his family after the failure of the '45, is an exciting and attractive man. Our chief narrator Mackellar, then, in his own sympathies is "intimately mingled" with the family saga and his psychological state and presentation of events are very interesting in their own right in the novel.

A Game of Honour and Evil

James, the heir to Durrisdeer, demonstrates a cool and cruel disposition as he forces the issue that a coin should be tossed to decide which of the brothers should go off to support the Stuarts:

> "It is the direct heir of Durrisdeer that should ride by his king's bridle," says the Master.
> "If we were playing a manly part," says Mr. Henry, "there might be sense in such talk. But what are we doing? Cheating at cards!"

"We are saving the house of Durrisdeer, Henry,"
his father said.

"And see, James," said Mr. Henry, "if I go, and the
Prince has the upper hand, it will be easy to make
your peace with King James. But if you go, and the
expedition fails, we divide the right and the title.
And what shall I be then?"

"You will be Lord Durrisdeer," said the Master. "I
put all I have upon the table."

"I play at no such game," cries Mr. Henry. "I shall
be left in such a situation as no man of sense and
honour could endure. I shall be neither fish nor
flesh!" he cried.

And a little after he had another expression,
plainer perhaps than he intended. "It is your duty to
be here with my father," said he. "You know well
enough you are the favourite."

"Ay?" said the Master. "And there spoke Envy!
Would you trip up my heels – Jacob?" said he, and
dwelled upon the name maliciously. (pp.12-13)

The master, James, seemingly speaks in his first utterance here
as a man of principle and honour. Henry reminds him, however, of
the pragmatism that the family is exercising in dividing its
loyalty in the first place and is dismissive of this tack utilising the
idea that they are merely "cheating at cards." James deliberately
throws this metaphor back in Henry's face by saying that he puts
all he has "upon the table" and so sardonically acknowledges his
part in a game. Henry rightly says that if James goes and the
Jacobites fail then the younger brother will be seen by others to
lack honour. He is provoked by the stubborn James and the
largely ineffectual though indulgent part that their father plays
in the conversation, and points out the brutal reality that James
is the brother Lord Durrisdeer would least like to lose. Clearly
winning the moral argument and displaying his own genuine
heroism, Henry is attacked by James for being envious and is
compared to the biblical Jacob who tricked his way to family
seniority. This insidious undermining of Henry by James allows
the situation to proceed to deciding matters on the toss of a coin.
We notice several aspects in this scenario that begin to establish
James as a Satanic figure. First of all there is his general levity,
his "devil may care" attitude, in treating the whole issue as a
game. Related to James's offer to gamble with Henry for the
outcome of their fates we have another Satanic resonance in the

idea of the taboo of bargaining or gambling with the devil. (Henry's ultimate miserable fate in the novel makes sense at least on the surface, in this folk-fashion, since he has been foolish in trucking with the devil and allowing the coin to be tossed). We see also another aspect of James's diabolism in his metaphoric shape-changing and his implicit projecting onto his brother of his own moral self; this is apparent in James calling his brother "Jacob" (ironically, another form of "James") and generally imputing to his brother his own sinfulness. We might actually read James as the envious one in the exchange above since he is determined to go off on a Jacobite adventure so as to appear the hero while it is Henry, as James resentfully realises, who is genuinely brave in embracing the logic that is best for all the family.

It seems that James's black-heartedness precedes the bitterness he feels when the Jacobite rebellion goes awry and he is outlawed and disinherited from his father's estate. He may well have been communing with the smugglers around his father's estate prior to this, and he shows and, indeed, utilises contempt for his brother to ensure that he is allowed to rally to the Stuart cause. He is predisposed toward evil, then, or is, even, motiveless evil. We might notice his repeated pattern of immorality in tossing a coin when he also uses this method to determine whether he and the Chevalier Burke should be friends or enemies. This predisposition is not unlike the source of evil in the Satan of Milton's epic poem *Paradise Lost* (1667) with whom James is compared in the novel. Milton's Satan rebels out of boredom, or simply because he can. James is perhaps just that kind of human being who is drawn to badness, something for which there is no complex explanation. Again we might recall the intellectual context surrounding *Jekyll and Hyde* where Darwin's idea of evolution perhaps allowed Stevenson to open up the idea of degeneration back down the evolutionary scale towards sheer animal wilfulness. Very subtly, however, drawing upon the recognisable mode of adventure and carrying, as it does, a number of strong echoes of Biblical situation, the novel allows a certain amount of psychological interpretation.

James Durie, the Prodigal Son

A good combination of immediately recognisable story and psychological resonance is the novel's embedded narrative of "The Prodigal Son." This is one of a number of places where we see Stevenson picking up the traces of a pre-existing story that exists deeply and extensively in the collective consciousness of the

audience or readership. Stevenson's contemporary and subsequent readership, culturally conditioned by their knowledge of
Christianity, recognise the prodigal son narrative. However, the
Christian idea behind this biblical parable, that of God, or the
father's infinite forgiveness, is one that rings in rather hollow
fashion in *The Master of Ballantrae*. Indeed, the novel is almost
anti-Christian in yoking together, as it does, the most spectacular
rebel from the father, Satan, and the prodigal son of Christ's
parable. In this welter of contradictory conflated Biblical
reference is, in fact, what we would recognise today as a strongly
Freudian pattern where the law of the jungle or "dog eat dog"
(even within the family set-up) is emphasised. This undercutting
of familiar Biblical texts makes, perhaps, for a suitably
uncomfortable reading experience of the novel. As these texts are
re-used, we might find ourselves appreciating the possible
psychological motivations behind the actions of James. Perhaps
his behaviour is related to the weakness of his father, not simply
because Lord Durrisdeer is so indulgent towards James but
because James is being over-zealous in playing what he takes to
be an active, manly part in reaction to the indolence and family
mismanagement in the father. The family, for rather shadowy
reasons, is in a state of dissolution prior to James's severance
from it. His watchword of "honour" may be a result of his
awareness, which he never explicitly admits, that his family
honour has been compromised. James, then, might be read as
shamed, angry and generally damaged by his family's situation. If
this is the case, then he emerges as, arguably, a self-hating and
self-destructive figure as opposed to inexplicable evil. We return
to the question posed in the preface: are we dealing with a
melodramatic or a deeply psychological situation?

James's Diabolic Role Playing
James is, at times, a melodramatic or stage-devil figure. We see
this in his terrorising of Wully White the Wabster who has told
tales of James's misdemeanours and has revenge visited upon him
by James's noises down the chimney, which Wully takes for an evil
visitation. We see his cheap tricks also as he conveniently forgets
his sense of honour to flee from the feisty character from
Stevenson's *Kidnapped*, Alan Breck Stewart, when the two come
into conflict. James knows he can run off and not have this
incident reported because within the strict code of the genuinely
honourable Stewart, the latter would appear foolish in the face of
a farcically exploding duel. We might note here that James is

precisely an anti-hero, a character that operates to subvert the conventions of the adventure story. Here again, as with the Bible stories that Stevenson draws upon, we see misfiring narratives where the expectations of the reader are entertained and disappointed, or even mocked. Might it be that Stevenson is saying that the stories that humans tell are often much less straightforward than they appear? If we are to follow this reading *The Master of Ballantrae*, in *Jekyll and Hyde* fashion, diagnoses a gap between outward, rational appearance and hidden psychological reality. We might back this idea up by observing that James is the favourite of the pious old family servant, John Paul, when we might expect him to prefer Henry; and that the old drunkard, Maconochie, takes the side of Henry when James might be expected to be more amenable to the irresponsible man. What are we to make of this disjunction? Is it the case that humans are psychologically attracted to their opposites?

James's role-playing is stereotypically caddish. Is he a one-dimensional rogue, or is it part of his cunning (his "master-plan") so to appear? We have a hint of deep design when we see his dealings with the pirates in the memoir of the Chevalier Burke. Here James usurps Captain Teach and instils discipline in the pirates and it is as though he wishes their evil to be an art. A similar question arises to those raised above, then: to what extent is James out of control, or, alternatively, is he all too malignly in control? Chevalier Burke delivers three letters from James to his family and we never learn the contents of these epistles. The main point, however, is that James wishes to work on each member of the family separately rather than explain himself in one go to these. The implication is that there is actually nothing to explain. For James the letters are simply props in his performance, both a means of continuing to sow division among his family and a means of obscuring the truth. James, it might be argued, is a man of much less substance and ability than he pretends. Ironically this lack of fibre is evident on his return from the failed rebellion after a long absence. His purpose is to worm his way back in with most of the family, but secretly to torment his brother so that a duel is ultimately precipitated:

> "Henry Durie," said the Master, "two words before I begin. You are a fencer, you can hold a foil; you little know what a change it makes to hold a sword! And by that I know you are to fall. But see how strong is my situation! If you fall, I shift out of this country to

> where my money is before me. If I fall, where are you?
> My father, your wife – who is in love with me, as you
> very well know – your child even, who prefers me to
> yourself: – how will these avenge me! Had you
> thought of that, dear Henry?" He looked at his brother
> with a smile; then made a fencing-room salute. (p.109)

We might expect the man of honour or chivalry (as James is so
often intent upon appearing) would simply proceed straight to
action in the duel, or at least use words to commend the bravery of
an opponent about to engage him. James, however, continues to
torment Henry, perhaps demonstrating his own insecurity and
seeking to gain an unfair advantage by depressing his opponent.
He claims that he will certainly win the fight and implies that the
House of Durrisdeer will then lie in ruins with Henry's death and
his own flight from the country. Even if Henry were the victor he
would simply accrue opprobrium from the family for having slain
the brother whom they all prefer. In fact, James loses the duel and
Henry dissolves in grief as he supposes his brother dead and
admits the episode to his father:

> With a broken, strangled cry, Mr. Henry leaped up
> and fell on his father's neck,crying and weeping, the
> most pitiful sight that ever a man witnessed. "O!
> father," he cried , "you know I loved him; you know I
> loved him in the beginning; I could have died for him
> – you know that! I would have given my life for him
> and you. O! say you know that. O! say you can
> forgive me. O, father, father, what have I done –
> what have I done? And we used to be bairns
> together!" and wept and sobbed, and fondled the old
> man, and clutched him about the neck, with a
> passion of a child in terror. (p.122)

We see here James's diabolic effect as he has engineered
transference of his own role as the prodigal son on to Henry.
Henry begs forgiveness from the father and reverts to the helpless
persona of a child. This is perhaps indicative that he and James
also to some extent have been denied a truly loving childhood by a
cold parent. Lord Durrisdeer reacts to Henry's agitation "like a
cold, kind spectator with his wits about him" (p.122), according to
our narrator and witness, Mackellar. Here we may have an
instance of Mackellar's unreliability: he is perhaps right about his
lordship's coldness, but wrong, we might well infer, in attributing

this state to paternal indulgence. His lordship is perhaps not so much "kind" as he is frozen with horror in the face of Henry's expression of genuine love both for his brother and his father. Lord Durrisdeer terminates this scene by saying to Mackellar, "We may leave him to his wife now" (p.122), which again might look like careful and ordered family management, but speaks, more likely, of Lord Durrisdeer being keen to escape the personally uncomfortable situation.

Henry Durie, a Man Mentally Stretched
James and Henry Durie are yoked together as brothers in conflict, but this conflicted existence perhaps does not pertain simply to the power-struggle that we witness in the central events of the novel. Lord Durisdeer's parenting has been negligent, as he has sat in isolation by the chimney reading his books and effectively demitting responsibility over both his sons. This leads to James's own disregard for responsibility and authority and to Henry's arguably over-anxious, and even prissy, attention to duty. Even before James has gone off on his Jacobite adventure, Henry attempts to manage the family estate, and so shoulders burdens more properly belonging to his father and brother. Henry is forbearing for the sake of his family, knowing full well that he takes second place to James in the affections not only of his father but also of Alison, the woman he marries anyway out of love and an attempt to secure the future of the family. He is also, as we have seen, not lacking in courage, both in trying to insist that he should fight for the Stuarts and in his duel with his brother. Henry, then, is a man of some moral and physical accomplishment and so we might well expect to see him in other circumstances as the emerging hero. As the novel progresses, however, we find a man mentally stretched and made darker by the strain of his persecutions. James, returned from his adventures, demands money from his brother and Henry's response, observed by Mackellar, represents the first in a series of moments of extreme emotional outburst:

> "Well, you shall see, and he shall see, and God shall
> see. If I ruin the estate and go barefoot, I shall stuff
> this bloodsucker. Let him ask all – all, and he shall
> have it! It is all his by rights. Ah!" he cried, "and I
> foresaw all this, and worse, when he would not let
> me go." (p.72)

Here Henry has a self-centred defiance that matches the habitual attitude of his brother. However understandable this might be in the context of the psychological duress under which Henry is placed, he goes so far as to contemplate the ruination of the family estate to which all his actions until now have seemingly been so opposed. Perhaps Henry here is a deep reader of his family situation, and is realising and commenting obliquely upon the fact that both his father and brother have been bringing about family ruination and that he might as well complete the process. In a moment of extreme stress, then, Henry is being defeatist about the prognosis for the Durrisdeers. Nonetheless, we witness yet again in a Durrisdeer male a self-destructive streak. There is the potential inference that all the males in the family-line are touched by hereditary instability and this combines with our knowledge that, mysteriously, the family later dies out to offer the possibility that we are dealing in the novel with a biological tragedy.

Henry gives into James's extortion even though it is such a drain on the estate. He perhaps does so out of a combination of love and guilt in the face of his older brother, even though James's plight is almost entirely self-made. Alternatively, there is fear in the actions of Henry in that he wishes to appease James so as to keep him away from Alison. As we see in the outburst quoted above, however, there is also the possibility that Henry acts out of anger and pride so that he claims, at this point, to value not even the estate above his sense of himself in the face of his brother's demands. This latter option represents curious reasoning on the part of Henry, suggesting that he would rather be defiantly compliant than show that the estate matters to him. Henry may be claiming the moral high ground by refusing to allow the thing to concern him. James for his part has only acted as though the estate is of importance to him when he is legally debarred from it. There is also perhaps a poetic justice operating where Henry ironically enough, and perhaps subconsciously, repeats the sin of his father in putting James before the estate.

Alison Durie, the Marginalised Female
The possibility of some congenital family mental illness is again hinted at with Henry's frequent bouts of illness after James's second disappearance following the duel. Typical of Stevenson's nicely nuanced structure, the supernatural connotation pertains so that Henry might be read as increasingly haunted by the devil or James. Henry, in his intermittent recovery from illness, is observed by Mackellar to turn to his wife "with all his emotions,

like a child to its mother" (p.133). It is as though a need is being expressed on Henry's part to break free from the predominantly male-dominated environment of his family. As in *Jekyll and Hyde*, there is a rather claustrophobic maleness in *The Master of Ballantrae*. Alison might be seen to conform to the criticism sometimes made of Stevenson that he is not particularly good at devising female characters. However, we could rather see her as in keeping with the world of business affairs and action as presented by the novel. The female is scarcely thought upon except, perhaps, as she brings to the male world ornamentation and, in the case of Alison, financial advantage. As Henry's decline into melancholy continues it should be noted that while he pays attention to his son and heir, he virtually ignores his daughter. Alison is sometimes an outspoken figure telling her husband prior to their marriage that she can bring him "pity" but not "love." At this point, both she and Henry know the reason for this forthrightness: she is in love with James. Alison, like Lord Durrisdeer, Mackellar, and Henry himself, pays testimony to the mysterious attractiveness exercised by James, even though it is doubtful if James ever has any real feelings for her, beyond her usefulness as an instrument with which he can torment the mind of his brother. As time goes by she comes to love Henry, though even then not passionately. Though a fairly lightly sketched character, she is historically true to the marginalised, silent female situation. In her initial honesty with Henry over her feelings for him and in her growing affection we see a strong character developing, but she can never take anything like a central role in the male-dominated world in which she exists.

Death in the Wilderness
Having fled to America with his family to escape his brother's attentions, Henry is, however, joined by James, who sets up as a tailor on the other side of the Atlantic and is intent on parading the irregular family history on the placard to his shop: "James Durie, Formerly Master of Ballantrae. Clothes Neatly Clouted" (p.199). This allows Henry, in fact, to usurp James's usual role as tormentor to some extent. Henry goes every day to sit on the bench beside James's business, a focal point from which the older brother deals with his customers. Henry cheerfully hails his acquaintances from this spot, saying that he is pleased to see his older brother at last gainfully employed and claiming that he is there in the capacity of an adviser. Henry tells the perturbed Mackellar of this scheme that, "I grow fat upon it" (p.201). The

vampirific connotation of this remark reverses the previous situation where James had something of the night about him as a "bloodsucker". Henry confidently claims with regard to his brother that he is "breaking his spirit" (p.201), but while he is partially successful in outplaying James, his prediction proves to be entirely overconfident, as we see in James's "sporting" acceptance of defeat:

> "Henry," said he, "I have for once made a false step, and for once you have had the wit to profit by it. The farce of the cobbler ends to-day; and I confess to you (with my compliments) that you have had the best of it. Blood will out; and you have certainly a choice idea of how to make yourself unpleasant." (p.202)

How are we to read this scenario? Perhaps Henry, for once, has trumped James and the latter is merely putting a good face upon things? Much darker, however, is the possibility that the triumph belongs, in fact, to James who has succeeded in bending his brother's behaviour to become exactly like his own. The devil works by encouraging bad behaviour, and Henry's remark about "growing fat" on his scheme is double-edged, carrying the possible connotation not only of a healthy fight back but also of being fattened up by the devil as meat for eventual slaughtering.

The deaths of the two brothers happening almost simultaneously in the American wilderness bring the plot to an end. Secundra Dass, James's (Asian) Indian companion is an exotic man, from a different world, whose attendance upon James again helps the latter hone his demonic image. The devil is often depicted as accompanied by minor demons, and Secundra's racial and "pagan" background and his seeming abilities as a fakir readily play to this notion. Secundra is engaged with James in a typically shoddy freebooting adventure with other brigands searching for treasure. He buries James after he has seemingly succumbed to illness, but is in fact seeking to wriggle free of his murderous colleagues. James, however, has been buried alive, having been taught by the Indian the technique of suspended animation. When Henry and Mackellar visit the grave with Secundra Dass some days later, the Indian disinters and attempts to revive James. For a moment, James's eyes open but the sight is too much for Henry who collapses dead on the spot. It is too late also for James, however, who has lain in the earth too long and cannot, in fact, be brought back to life. James's final attempt at sleight of hand diabolic invincibility goes personally wrong though not before it brings about the destruction of his brother. It is appropriate that James should die here also since the death of the object of his persecution brings to an end his *raison d'être*. The ending of the novel, then, is somewhat melodramatic, and points us perhaps toward the idea that the house of Ballantrae was all along too self-absorbed and brought about its own spectacular implosion.

Mackellar and his Narrative

Ephraim Mackellar, on the face of it, appears to be a rather dull character. He is, in James's eyes, "Square-toes", the dependable and pious Edinburgh MA educated in the puritanical atmosphere of the earlier eighteenth century. Even here though there is a potential ambiguity in that one might wonder why a man who has actually completed a degree does not go on to pursue a career in the Scottish church as would be probable at this time. It is not entirely clear how Mackellar has entered the service of the house of Durrisdeer, and there is the possible inference to be drawn that Mackellar's stewardship of a family in something of a dark and semi-ruinous state betokens some irregularity in his own background.

A more certain ambiguity in Mackellar's character is his penchant for constructing the romantic adventure story that he relates. We would not necessarily expect him to be drawn to poetic legend, given his Presbyterian demeanour, but early on in his narrative he cites appearances of the Durie family in old rhymes. For instance, "Kittle folk are the Durrisdeers,/They ride wi' ower mony spears" (p.9). At the same time, however, these lines might seem to the Calvinist in Mackellar to confirm the preordained fate of the family. The lines speak ostensibly of the family's potency, but also (in the phrase, "ower mony") suggest that their huge strength carries with it volatility (as the implosion of the family in the novel bears out). Overall however, Mackellar is at pains to construct the full drama of the story of the Durie brothers, even incorporating the memoirs of the Chevalier Burke so as to follow James's adventures abroad. For much of the novel Mackellar is too simply intent on chronicling James's often shoddy travails. He it is, arguably, who succumbs most easily to James's stage-Satanism and so helps create the texture of hysterical melodrama. We see Mackellar's susceptibility to James's presence at its highpoint after Henry has struck his brother: "The Master sprang to his feet like one transfigured; I had never seen the man so beautiful" (p.107). Is it the case that Mackellar here is fooled by James's theatricality or does he accurately register the great power which James derives from the negativity of others and which reinforces the supernatural texture of his character?

Mackellar claims eventually to see through James's personality. He seems to point towards the superficiality or crudity of James's methods: "It came upon me in a kind of vision how hugely I had overrated the man's subtlety" (p.159). Given James's tenacity, which Mackellar continues to describe, we might not be entirely convinced by this statement. Mackellar remains fascinated by the story of the two brothers, strangely affected by both. He is at his most intensely involved in the episode of the aborted murder attempt that he plans upon James at sea. It is very much as though he feels that he is possessed of a moral discernment which is frighteningly superior to the extent that he plots this murder. Does he represent a character too certain in his own mind in judging others? We might detect this even in his production of a story that often appears on the surface a melodramatic romance with a one-dimensional villain. Alternatively, does Mackellar, in fact, sum up the essential conflict when he says to James at one point, "Your brother is a good man, and you are a bad one – neither more nor less" (p.191). As with *Jekyll and Hyde*, *The Master of Ballantrae* asks questions about the depths and sources of human moral nature that remain uncomfortably ambiguous in the reader's mind throughout and to the end of the novel.

Notes
1. RLSCH, p.350
2. Ibid.

The Ebb-Tide (1894)

The action begins in nineteenth century Tahiti when three dysfunctional white drop-outs steal a schooner with the intention of sailing it to South America to sell off the cargo. When the scheme goes wrong, they make landfall on a mysterious island controlled by the fatalist missionary, Attwater. Their squalid treachery is easily outwitted by Attwater. One is killed and another finds religion. Having set fire to the abandoned ship, Herrick, the main protagonist seems ready to drift away into a hopeless future.

Mode and Setting

The Ebb-Tide started life in 1889 as a project by Stevenson's stepson, Lloyd Osbourne, and some debate continues as to the extent of their joint authorship. Osbourne has some claim to creating the material in the early chapters, but Stevenson expended much spirit-sapping energy polishing the final version and writing as a solo project well over half the book, including the tale of his renegade trio of protagonists at sea and on the mysterious island belonging to the sinister Attwater. In a letter to his friend Sidney Colvin, Stevenson summed up the effort the book had extracted from him while expressing satisfaction with "the tale"; he writes, "The devil himself would allow a man to brag a little after such a crucifixion!"[1] *The Ebb-Tide* remains a somewhat difficult reading experience due, perhaps, to its mixture of realism and allegory, a combination that many critics have found to sit somewhat discordantly. However, it is possible to argue that this dissonant combination represents yet another version, perhaps Stevenson's most accomplished rendition, of his sense of the duality of the human world. As with *The Strange Case of Dr Jekyll and Mr Hyde* and *The Master of Ballantrae*, *The Ebb-Tide* is a study of the human spirit degraded by evil action. Instead of the dark, winter settings of London and Scotland, however, this scenario is played out in the paradisial environment of the islands of the South Pacific. Constantly, the ideal, mythical setting of the novella clashes with the grimly ignoble human nature that is on display.

    The Ebb-Tide begins with the characters of Davis, Herrick and Huish "on the beach", or washed-up like so much shoreline detritus. Anticipating the fiction of Joseph Conrad, and after a

fashion in which only the then obscure Herman Melville among
Stevenson's contemporaries was operating, Stevenson casts a
withering eye upon the spread of "white civilisation":

> Throughout the island world of the Pacific, scattered
> men of many European races and from almost every
> grade of society carry activity and disseminate
> disease. Some prosper, some vegetate. Some have
> mounted the steps of thrones and owned islands and
> navies. Others again must marry for a livelihood; a
> strapping, merry, chocolate-coloured dame supports
> them in sheer idleness; and, dressed like natives, but
> still retaining some foreign element of gait or attitude,
> still perhaps with some relic (such as a single eye-
> glass) of the officer and gentleman, they sprawl in
> palm-leaf verandahs and entertain an island audience
> with memoirs of the music-hall. (p.123)

This passage that opens the book establishes the European
colonisers as grotesque, mutable plague carriers. As post-colonial
historians have increasingly realised, Europeans spread illness as
much as technology and culture throughout their colonies from the
seventeenth to the nineteenth centuries. Indeed, areas of the South
Seas witnessed the collapse of the native population due to their
biological inability to resist viruses brought by the white peoples.
Stevenson's opening also acknowledges the insidious facility of the
colonisers to "go native" by taking their "thrones", or assuming
"primitive" leadership and by becoming lazy, living off the efforts of
the native peoples (a nice reversal of the stereotype of the supposed
indolence of such primitive peoples is here incorporated by
Stevenson). We find here also the far from exalted art of the "music-
hall" which is the culture that the whites carry. The undermining of
the claims of superior, civilising influence traditionally made by
European colonialism is comprehensive in this passage and carries
with it connotations of the whites as parasitical.

A Trio of Drifters
The three drifters who have fallen in with one another all use
aliases...Davis, Herrick and Huish. As white men, they have become
particularly dispossessed. In the first chapter they are to be found
impoverished and hungry, sharing fantasies of their favourite meal.
Huish is suffering from influenza and they are driven from the beach
by rain and shelter in the old calaboose. Huddled together as
morning breaks, the state of the three perhaps leads the reader to

expect a tale to unfold where human fellowship is borne out of shared adversity. For breakfast they have fried bananas, obtained from the boat-crew of "kanakas", a word used by westerners for South Seas natives, who provide this bounty in return for Davis dancing to his own whistling accompaniment. Visibly as low as they can go, and afraid that the French controlling authorities are contemplating gaoling the drifters into forced labour, the trio embark upon the scheme of forming a crew for the *Farallone*, a vessel where the crew has been deprived of its white officers due to death from smallpox. In gaining permission to take command of the ship and its crew of blacks to complete its journey carrying champagne to Australia, the trio seem now to be socially ascending again. For fear that disease still lingers aboard, no other white crew can be persuaded to take on the mission of piloting the stricken ship, and so a daring opportunity presents itself to the three protagonists. Dynamics of rising and falling fortune, then, are embedded at the start of the novel, and we await to see if redemption is to be the lot of the three men.

We are also primed by the different roles that the three drifters occupy. Davis, an American sea-captain cast from his occupation for drunkenness now has the opportunity to reclaim his former role. Huish is invited to apply efficiency to overseeing the ship's cargo, for which his previous occupation as a clerk would seem to suit him. Less obviously of use in the venture of transporting the *Farallone* is Herrick, a university drop-out. He stands, on the face of it, archetypally for the culture of the west, sharing names with one of the classic English poets (Robert Herrick), and having a knowledge of French and of Virgil. The last of these resonances might make the reader think of Virgil's epic *Aeneid*, and wonder if Stevenson's Herrick also has it in him to undertake a momentous, heroic journey that will contrast with his initial state of degradation. The men seem to have been saved in time; as Herrick says, "Another week and I'd have murdered some one for a dollar" (p.160). Eating heartily aboard the *Farallone*, however, soon gives way to Davis and Huish drinking deeply from the ship's cargo. Herrick though demurs from dissolution and remains admirably "manly." It is only when his two comrades have drunk the first batch of the cargo and start on the second that they realise that most of the bottles of champagne have been filled with water and deduce that the owners of the ship are counting on losing it through their delinquency to cash in on the insurance. Yet again, then, we look for the three men to rise above their characters and to meet a poisoned challenge heroically. Davis proposes that they sink the boat near a place where there is an

American consul so that with his citizenship he and his colleagues can be shipped to San Francisco and out of their predicament entirely. He discovers, however, that their food is very low and seeks to blame the cook for waste. Huish points out, however, that Davis himself has been eating excessively and refuses to give credence to Davis's newfound sense of responsibility, which he is now expressing so haughtily. Violent dispute is prevented only when they happen upon a mysterious island, whose existence it seems is somewhat recorded in a sea manual of the South Seas from 1851. Yet again, the reader expects some definitive experience on the horizon as dangerous or enchanted island experiences in the *Aeneid*, Shakespeare's *The Tempest,* Daniel Defoe's *Robinson Crusoe* and Jonathan Swift's *Gulliver's Travels* might be recalled. But once more the grimy moral state of the drifters is to the fore as they are brought into collision with a mythical setting. Stevenson keeps the realism of the encountered scene and its foreboding resonances closely together. We see this as Herrick explores the stone houses on the shore:

> Therein were cables, windlasses, and blocks of every size and capacity; cabin windows and ladders; rusty tanks, a companion hatch; a binnacle with its brass mountings and its compass idly pointing, in the confusion and dusk of that shed, to a forgotten pole; ropes, anchors, harpoons, a blubber-dipper of copper, green with years, a steering-wheel, a tool-chest with the vessel's name upon the top, the *Asia*: a whole curiosity-shop of sea-curios, gross and solid, heavy to lift, ill to break, bound with brass and shod with iron. Two wrecks at the least must have contributed to this random heap of lumber; and as Herrick looked upon it, it seemed to him as if the two ships' companies were there on guard, and he heard the tread of feet and whisperings, and saw with the tail of his eye the commonplace ghosts of sailor men. (p.201)

From this catalogue of material solidity, Herrick imaginatively extracts "ghosts." The items he observes are obviously going to be salvaged by people living in such an isolated location, but Herrick's mind hints to him the idea of sirens and monsters wilfully luring seafarers to destruction and death. It is a passage that is emblematic of the debris, or rubbish of white civilisation, among which, most especially through Herrick's eyes, he and his two companions might be seen.

The Island's Overlord

The trio at this point have just been introduced to Attwater, the university educated Englishman who controls the mysterious island. On one level, this name is mundane sounding enough, but on another it carries a very obviously symbolic overtone; Attwater is an elemental name implying for Herrick and for the reader, perhaps, omnipotence within this seabound environment. On meeting Attwater, Davis resorts to the alias of "Brown" and Herrick to that of "Hay", with only Huish revealing his usual name. His habitual alias has, like Herrick's, been "Hay" but since he introduces himself after Herrick to Attwater he has no time to think of a new moniker. We expect, then, an unravelling of this low deceit in some dramatic collision with the island's overlord. Attwater himself moves in and out of the conventions of banal "English" politeness and a portentous persona that confuses both Herrick and the reader. He invites the trio to dinner:

> "Shall we say half-past six? *So* good of you!"
> His voice, in uttering these conventional phrases, fell at once into the false measure of society; and Herrick unconsciously followed the example, "I am sure we shall be very glad," he said. "At half-past six? Thank you so very much."
> "'For my voice has been tuned to the note of the gun That startles the deep when the combat's begun,'" quoted Attwater, with a smile, which instantly gave way to an air of funereal solemnity. (p.194)

We see here a familiar protean quality in Attwater as he rapidly moves between conventional politeness and a somewhat threatening quotation. He is, perhaps, making himself an island demon promising no good to the trio, and it is after this that he allows Herrick his conducted tour through the house with its detritus seemingly confirming in Herrick's mind that this is a place where people are lured to their destruction. Attwater tells the men of having buried twenty nine souls out of thirty three inhabitants on the island recently as a result of the small-pox. Herrick also notices that Davis is more silent and subdued than normal, dispensing with his habitually confident "skipper" persona and all of this contributes to his sense of Attwater's uncanny, presiding power. Attwater encourages the idea in Herrick's head that the island is enchanted. To Herrick's judgement that the island is "heavenly" (p.202), Attwater responds:

> "I daresay too, you can appreciate what one calls it.
> It's a lovely name. It has a flavour, it has a colour, it
> has a ring and fall to it; it's like its author – it's half
> Christian! Remember your first view of the island,
> and how it's only woods and woods and water; and
> suppose you had asked somebody for the name, and
> he had answered – *nemorosa Zacynthos*' [from Virgil's
> *Aeneid* – "now shady Zacynthos appears in the middle
> of the flood"]. (p.202)

Again, then, Attwater maintains the uncertain state in Herrick's
mind between reality and myth, and he extends this dubiety into
the notion of the island's name being (like Virgil, appropriated in
Christian times as proto-Christian in his world outlook) "half-
Christian." Attwater himself, like Virgil, might appear half-pagan,
a Greek God secure in his own domain who vengefully punishes
those who complain about their fates. This resonance of ungrateful
human beings, complaining against and summoned before a
classical God is nicely set up earlier in the novel as Huish,
unhappy at sea with Davis, ejaculates, "Blow me, if it ain't enough
to make a man write an insultin' letter to Gawd!" (p.182-3). The
notion of hubristic sinning against the Gods in tragedy is planted,
then, in the alert reader's mind, which is increasingly primed for
the unfolding of a classical denouement as the novel proceeds.
    Attwater though is also a Victorian Christian missionary, who
censoriously demands that Herrick pays attention to:

> "He who upholds you, He whom you daily crucify
> afresh? There is nothing here," – strikes on his bosom
> – "nothing there" – smiting the wall – "and nothing
> there" – stamping – "nothing but God's Grace! We
> walk upon it, we breathe it; we live and die by it; it
> makes the nails and axles of the universe ..." (p.203)

Attwater here enunciates a traditional enough Christian
conception: that every universal and human action is accounted
for in the divine economy; our responses to any situation, however
unpropitious, should be morally righteous. Yet again the idea of
redemption is brought into the narrative, most especially for
Herrick, the only one of the trio who is engaged by Attwater's
disquisitions. Attwater's evangelical fervour, however, where he is
physically as well as verbally engaged in rendering The Word,
might put us on our guard that he is a fanatic. His certainty, or
charged Christian realism, which involves manipulating the

atheist Herrick's mind so that he sees the island as both "heavenly" and a place altogether more sinister, contrasts with the younger man's uncertainty, and as the pair are drawn to one another, we might realise that once again in Stevenson's oeuvre we are dealing with two opposite extremes.

Attwater and the Prodigal Son
Davis and Huish hatch a plan to murder Attwater and to take control of what his island has to offer, most especially in the way of pearls. They seek to put Attwater at a false sense of ease at the dinner to which the island's overlord invites the trio. Typically Stevenson, as he describes Attwater, insinuates the question of how much in control of events the plotters are:

> A cat of huge growth sat on his shoulder purring, and occasionally, with a deft paw, capturing a morsel in the air. To a cat he might be likened himself, as he lolled at the head of his table, dealing out attentions and innuendos, and using the velvet and the claw indifferently. And both Huish and the captain fell progressively under the charm of his hospitable freedom. (p.212)

The simile here of Attwater toying with his prey is obvious enough. If Attwater is a metaphor for the God who controls human destiny, we see a very dubious figure that gratuitously enchants human beings though with nasty ends in mind for them. We come close at this point to a sense of Stevenson's own atheism, though one charged, perhaps, with the Calvinist sensibility of his upbringing. Humans enjoy the world at their peril, because their experiences inevitably end in the disappointment of death. At this point, for all that Herrick has not renounced his atheism, he has a strong sense that Attwater can see through the murderous plot and will prevail. The underlying psychology of the scenario, however, is that Herrick also bears in mind the impression of the habitual ineptitude of his erstwhile comrades and believes that any of their schemes to better their lot are bound to go awry.

In an effort to evade Attwater and the whole tense situation, Herrick hurls abuse at him in response to the overlord's story of shooting in cold blood a black servant who has plotted against a colleague who as a result committed suicide. Herrick's action here is one of genuine revulsion and fear, but it shows him also trying not to interfere with forces more powerful than himself. He suggests that he and Davis, who has followed him as he stormed away from Attwater's stone house, should flee, leaving behind the odious determined Huish to attempt the life of Attwater: "Where to, my son?" said the captain. "Up anchor's easy saying. But where to?" "To sea," responded Herrick. "The sea's big enough! To sea – away from this dreadful island and that, oh! that sinister man!" (p.221). Herrick here wants to disappear again into the obscurity of the ocean, away from attempts to impose one's own will upon life. He tries to explain to Davis that Attwater, with his Christian zeal, has a sense of purpose that the trio of drifting, habitual failures cannot match. He tells Davis that Attwater is a fatalist:

> "What's that, a fatalist?" said Davis.
> "Oh, it's a fellow that believes a lot of things," said Herrick, "believes that his bullets go true; believes that all falls out as God chooses, do as you like to prevent it; and all that."
> "Why, I guess I believe right so myself," said Davis.
> "You do?" said Herrick.
> "You bet I do!" says Davis.
> Herrick shrugged his shoulders. "Well, you must be a fool," said he, and he leaned his head upon his knees.
> (p.222)

Here we see part of a pattern in *The Ebb-Tide*, that of the search for and disappointment with the father-figure in Herrick's life. We have heard early on in the novel that Herrick is a son to "an intelligent, active, and ambitious man" (p.125) whose London business goes bankrupt, forcing the father to "begin the world again as a clerk" (p.125). With his own future considerably foreclosed by the father's misfortune, Herrick becomes prodigal, so that "his career thenceforth was one of unbroken shame" (p.125). His attempts, as prodigal son to return to the father, include his attraction to Davis, whose own ruinous career, it gradually emerges, has included causing the drowning of others at sea owing to his drunkenness aboard the *Sea Ranger*. Davis is a man like Herrick's father who has been thrust to the bottom of the world and he resembles him quite precisely in his level of misfortune. We find here a typical Stevensonian technique of running narratives from the Bible where these are suggestive but ultimately pallid versions of Christian stories. This operation is in keeping with the generally sceptical, withering outlook on western culture so often wielded by Stevenson.

Herrick is dismayed by Davis's expression of his own "fatalism", his belief in big stories and big controlling hands to the extent of calling Davis "a fool", but Davis is not to be dissuaded from his big story or plan against Attwater. Before this can be put into action, however, the overlord of the island has ambushed the two, bringing with him the now very drunken Huish who has let slip the real names of the trio along with something of their true history and so aroused suspicion:

> "There is your Whitechapel carrion!" said Attwater.
> "And now you might very well ask me why I do not
> put a period to you at once, as you deserve. I will tell
> you why, Davis. It is because I have nothing to do
> with the *Sea Ranger* and the people you drowned, or
> the *Farallone* and the champagne that you stole.
> That is your account with God; He keeps it, and He
> will settle it when the clock strikes. In my own case,
> I have nothing to go on but suspicion, and I do not
> kill on suspicion, not even vermin like you. But
> understand! if ever I see any of you again, it is
> another matter, and you shall eat a bullet. And now
> take yourself off." (p.224)

Attwater here, for all his Christian zeal that many will find unattractive, acts with a strong sense of justice. He refuses to play God to the extent that Herrick might well have expected, even though his moral estimation of the men is sure enough. After returning to the *Farallone* again and lapsing into despair at being judged among the "vermin" once again, Herrick attempts suicide by drowning but fails even in this. He is cast ashore where he is found by Attwater, and, in one of the most shocking moments in the novel, he throws himself on the overlord's mercy:

> "Here I am. I am broken crockery; I am a burst
> drum; the whole of my life is gone to water; I have
> nothing left that I believe in, except my living horror
> of myself. Why do I come to you? I don't know; you
> are cold, cruel, hateful; and I hate you, or I think I
> hate you. But you are an honest man, an honest
> gentleman. I put myself, helpless, in your hands.
> What must I do? If I can't do anything, be merciful
> and put a bullet through me; it's only a puppy with a
> broken leg!" (p.230)

For Herrick, Attwater represents a certainty of action that contrasts with the weak drifting of the trio. The symbolism is overt as the name Attwater stands for a fullness at odds with the weak water, or the "ebb-tide", of the three drifters. Once again, then, we find Stevenson setting up a rather heavily underlined opposition. However, in this emphatic, ironically oppositional manner Stevenson, arguably, signals that Attwater's sense of purpose is not to be taken any more seriously than the lack of real purpose displayed by the trio. The atheist Herrick begins to worship a false god in Attwater who stands for the firm white hand in the South Seas and elsewhere, colonising, controlling and proselytising to the native peoples. He is an ambiguous figure, the nearest in this novel to a demon. Amidst the welter of false certainty that Herrick pours out is his quasi-biblical series of metaphors where he describes himself as "broken crockery" and "a burst drum". Added to this is the strong overtone yet again of the prodigal son, and also his rebaptism through the element of water in his aborted suicide and his request to Attwater for some kind of redemption. If his case is hopelessly irredeemable, however, he asks that Attwater should kill him there and then. His surrender to the lay preacher at this point is so complete that he pictures himself as "only a puppy with a broken leg" and this indicates his complete submission. Even as Herrick has capitulated however, in adopting so complete a set of terms of Christian sinfulness and submission, we might suspect that he is losing his mind and, indeed, his plea to be put down like an animal represents self-abnegation gone too far.

Failed Narratives and the Confederacy of Selfishness
As indicated already, *The Ebb-Tide* is a novel where expectations, of redemption, of South Seas adventure perhaps, are set up and then disappointed. This is true also for Attwater described in orthodox folk-terminology by Herrick as "sinister" and so seen as demonic, but then appears to the young man as a saviour-figure in the passage last quoted. The reader finds a similarly slippery experience in the reading of Herrick's character, where we perhaps keep expecting that he might emerge as a hero, or at least win through to some kind of principled stance that we can respect. Herrick is both cultured and thoughtful and we expect also that he will make some kind of sense of the situation he is in. His capitulation to Attwater, however, seems shockingly, childishly retrogressive. (It parallels the scene in *The Master of Ballantrae* where Henry dissolves in grief after he supposes

himself to have killed his brother.) He has stopped thinking at
this point and has given himself up wholly to someone else's
vision of order. Herrick seems to accept Attwater's ability put
things right though what this means in practice precisely is
unclear, even to Herrick himself. It is as though he is acting a role,
that of the prodigal son or the image of the penitent bequeathed to
him by his culture. He inhabits this posture, perhaps, out of sheer
frustration and exhaustion in the face of his life; he surrenders
himself to it, something that is registered in the hysterical extent
to which he pursues his obeisance.

As with Herrick's capitulation to Attwater, there is something
rather stilted, or too neat, about the sub-title of the novel, "A Trio
and a Quartette", which defines the two parts of the novel. We
might take the first section in its focusing upon a "trio" as
indicating that Stevenson is moving beyond the dualism of the
portrayal of human nature in *Jekyll and Hyde* to read multiform
selfishness and fragmentation in human society. The idea of a
"trio" might make the reader think of an esprit de corps (as in "the
three musketeers", perhaps), but we find that the coming together
of the sly, self-seeking Huish, the vane, clubbable Davis and the
aimless, cultured drifter Herrick is a situation of convenience.
Each of them recognises in his companions skills or abilities that
he himself does not possess, and in pooling their talents they
intuit that their collectivity might be put to use in allowing them
slyly to negotiate life. All three are aware that there is some
deceit or dark past in the situation of their companions, and this
is the one thing, rather than any real camaraderie, that they have
binding them together. One can read this scenario as emblematic
of Stevenson's depressing outlook on the reality of human society
as a confederacy of selfishness.

When the trio becomes a "quartette" (carrying with it the
ironic association of a harmonious string ensemble, one of the
ornaments of civilisation), things become particularly tense. False
bonhomie excruciatingly exudes from the first meeting of the
three adventurers with Attwater:

> "Well," said Davis, "I suppose you may call it an
> accident. We had heard of your island, and read that
> thing in the Directory about the *Private Reasons*, you
> see; so when we saw the lagoon reflected in the sky, we
> put her head for it at once, and so here we are."
> "'Ope we don't intrude!" said Huish.
> The stranger looked at Huish with an air of faint

surprise, and looked pointedly away again. It was
hard to be more offensive in dumb show. "It may suit
me, your coming here," he said. "My own schooner is
overdue, and I may put something in your way in the
meantime. Are you open to a charter?"

"Well I guess so," said Davis; "it depends."

"My name is Attwater," continued the stranger,
"You, I presume, are the captain?"

"Yes, sir. I am the captain of this ship: Captain
Brown," was the reply. "Well, see 'ere!" said Huish,
"better begin fair! 'E's skipper on deck right enough,
but not below. Below, we're all equal, all got a lay in
the adventure; when it comes to business, I'm as
good as 'e; and what I say is, let's go into the 'ouse
and have a lush, and talk it over among pals. We've
got some prime fizz," he said, and winked.

The presence of the gentleman lighted up like a
candle the vulgarity of the Clerk; and Herrick
instinctively, as one shields himself from pain, made
haste to interrupt." (pp.192-3)

Davis struggles at the outset of this intercourse to justify the
landing on Attwater's island. He calls their arrival an "accident",
even although he acknowledges that they have been studying
their sea-manual for somewhere to land and have done so here, in
spite of their briefing that it is a private place. Immediately, then,
he conveys the essential aimlessness, desperation and "vulgarity"
of their voyage. Huish's cockney accented intervention at this
point with the social nicety of " 'ope we don't intrude" confirms to
the snobbish Attwater the crassness of the new arrivals. His
returned silence counterpoints the falsity of the babble of Davis
and Huish. He follows this with a test, enquiring if they might be
chartered, and the vague and uncertain responses of Davis and
Huish (with Huish claiming that there exists aboard the
Farallone no actual, ordered hierarchy) confirms Attwater's
suspicions that he is dealing with a gang of freebooters. Herrick
observes all this in social horror, realising what a poor show they
are making. Implicit here is a dark comedy as in the "wilds" of the
South Seas Attwater and Herrick respond to the social niceties of
their shared Oxbridge background. Attwater is not himself an
unmottled character. He seems ridiculous in having named his
own schooner *Trinity Hall* after his university college. He has
been waiting for its arrival but instead of such a sublime,
symbolically civilised nautical visitation, he receives the shabby
Farallone with its dysfunctional trio. If Attwater is Godlike on his

island (at least in the eyes of Herrick), he is perhaps mocked at this point by Stevenson in his defeated expectations of what is arriving from the sea. Attwater apparently maintains the veneer of civilisation on his island, but his autocratic overlordship of the small group of natives and his sometimes impassioned, evangelical ejaculations, speak of a primitive brutality that contradicts his conceit of white civilisation.

It seems clear that the scenario for the quartette is to be no better than that of the trio. Herrick had previously added to the graffiti in the old Papeete prison a quotation from Virgil to the effect: "O thrice and four time blest, whose fate it was to die before their fathers' eyes beneath the high walls of Troy" (p.144). Stevenson's use of this citation is sardonic as it refers to humans being blest by the gods in their tragic fates. The old epics like Virgil's *Aeneid*, bulwarks of western civilisation, speak of heroes achieving fitting outcomes for their peoples through heroic deeds. *The Ebb-Tide*, however, mocks the idea of ordered fate: it is a novel where the idea of heroic deeds and action are viewed witheringly. Both the trio and quartette sections offer falsified versions of events, where no good or decisive outcome can be expected. We see a good, ironic example of the falsity of ordered narratives when after at first being foiled in his plan to murder Attwater, Huish considers his second attempt to be like the battle between David and Goliath and the chapter in which this happens takes the biblical pairing for its title. Huish is, of course, a very unattractive version of the Jewish hero, David, conquering the smug giant, Goliath against all the odds. It is significant that the most distasteful character in the novel, Huish, should entertain the notion, not at all ironically, that he is cast into the chivalrous role in his proposed one-to-one combat with Attwater. Even he entertains the notion of a grand story written into his life on occasion, just as Attwater reads providence or the will of God in the world, and as Davis carries the notion of his grand rehabilitation as a mariner. Herrick, on the face of it, would seem quite explicitly to be the individual amongst the quartette the least attached to belief that there is a meaningful story running through his life. He seems to be pointedly avoiding making anything of himself, although his letter home to Emma (his former love) in Britain affects a romantic pose. Given Herrick's attachment to Virgil's epic adventure, his taste for German music, and most tellingly perhaps, his name's association with the lyric poet, Robert Herrick, it might be that he too is constructing an image or story of himself as a romantic wastrel turning his back on a comfortable life. We are told that he has been dissolute, but we do not know the details of any sins or crimes committed. The possibility is that he may be on the run as a result of the enormity of these, and that he is retrospectively constructing an image of himself as self-outcast. We do not even know if Emma, a rather stereotypical, literary moniker for a lover, actually exists. The reader is surprised to find Herrick embracing Attwater's version of the Christian story when he surrenders to him, but this episode perhaps merely confirms Herrick's propensity for grand narrative all along.

Narratives, or stories, ultimately fail in *The Ebb-Tide*. The process starts with the undermining of the adventure setting of the South Seas, revealing its rancid underbelly of white indolence and disease. The cast of liars and cheats includes not only the trio, but also the supposedly respectable owners of the *Farallone* who murderously conspire to lose their capital to swindle the insurance. Unsurprisingly, but with black comedy, David (or Huish) is defeated by Goliath (Attwater), and a final chapter sees Attwater have the *Farallone* burned as the *Trinity Hall* comes in sight to take Davis and Herrick off the island. Curiously, as the novel ends, Davis is praying fervently, seemingly having become, in Herrick's words, "Attwater's spoiled darling and pet penitent" (p.252). What has happened? The persistent dreamer and self-deluder, Davis, has bought into Attwater's vision of sinful man and the need for punishment and repentance, while for Herrick, the romantic ne'er-do-well, his "conversion" has worn off. Davis is reluctant to leave; he has become institutionalised in a short time to the comfort or (Christian) prison of Attwater's island, while the drifter Herrick is now quite happy to leave, drifting off to wherever life will next take him.

Plain Unvarnished Existence
How, finally, are we to make any overall sense of *The Ebb-Tide*, a text that is full of strange and contradictory events, and which Stevenson admits he spent huge mental effort working out? There is no very neat symbolic story for us to interpret; instead the novel lurches between stories that are all too claustrophobically neat (such as Herrick's seeming conversion by Attwater), and sequences of events where the logical connections are far from clear. We might say that *The Ebb-Tide* is something of a proto-Existentialist text. Existentialism, as a philosophy, is strongly associated with the first half of the twentieth century, most famously in the work of Jean Paul Sartre, but, as so often,

4

Stevenson is prescient of the intellectual currents that are just around the corner of his own age. Existentialism identifies mankind as alone in a godless universe, and with this realisation goes the difficult burden (indeed, in psychological terms, the anxiety) of making choices for oneself. No-one has a life which is predetermined; there is no pre-existing niche for any individual and no ultimate metaphysical or spiritual ending. Human significance is not suffused with universal values, but is instead realistically significant in the moment-to-moment texture of experience (or existence), and it is up to the "authentic" individual to live each moment honestly and with free-will. *The Ebb-Tide* features a cast, in Existential terms, of "inauthentic" characters, all of whom, at certain points, are being evasive and constructing false versions of themselves and their lives. Ultimately, the novel shows us a rather primitive world where the protagonists drown in a surfeit of shoddy stories and adventures and where human beings find it difficult to face up to their plain, unvarnished existence.

Notes
1. *RLSCH,* p.451.

Robert Louis Stevenson: Select Bibliography

The editions of Stevenson's novels chosen for citation throughout this work have been selected for their textual reliability as well as being conveniently available editions.

Biographies
Bell, Ian, *Robert Louis Stevenson: Dreams of Exile*. Mainstream: Edinburgh, 1992. *The most readable treatment of RLS.*

Calder, Jenni, *RLS: A Life Study*. Hamish Hamilton: London, 1980.

Callow, Philip, *Louis: A Life of Robert Louis Stevenson*. Constable: London, 2001.

McLynn, Frank, *Robert Louis Stevenson*. Hutchinson: London, 1993. *The most thorough biography of RLS.*

General Studies
Calder, Jenni (ed), *Stevenson and Victorian Scotland*. Edinburgh University Press, 1981.

Chesterton, G.K., *Robert Louis Stevenson*. Hodder & Stoughton: London, 1927.

Eigner, Edwin, *Robert Louis Stevenson and the Romantic Tradition*. Princeton University Press, 1966.

Hammond, J.R., *A Robert Louis Stevenson Companion: A Guide to the Novels, Essays and Short Stories*. MacMillan: London, 1984.

Hillier, Robert Irwin, *The South Seas Fiction of Robert Louis Stevenson*. Peter Lang: New York, 1989.

Kiely, Robert, *Robert Louis Stevenson and the Fiction of Adventure*. Harvard University Press: Cambridge MA, 1965.

Maixner, Paul (ed), *Robert Louis Stevenson: The Critical Heritage*. Routledge & Kegan Paul: London, Boston & Henley, 1981. *A superbly judicious collection of mostly contemporary critical response to the work of RLS.*

Noble, Andrew (ed), *Robert Louis Stevenson*. Vision and Barnes & Noble: London & Totowa NJ, 1983.

Sandison, Alan, *Robert Louis Stevenson and the Appearance of Modernism*. Macmillan: Basingstoke, 1995.

Terry, R.C. (ed), *Robert Louis Stevenson: Interviews and Recollections*. Macmillan: Basingstoke, 1996. *A very useful collection of sources.*

The Strange Case of Dr Jekyll and Mr Hyde
Edition:
The Strange Case of Dr Jekyll and Mr Hyde and Other Tales of Terror edited by Robert Mighall (Penguin: London, 2002).

General studies of the double in literature:
Keppler, C.F., The Literature of the Second Self. University of
  Arizona Press: Tucson, 1972.
Miller, Karl, *Doubles: Studies in Literary History.* Oxford
  University Press, 1985.
Rogers, Robert, *A Psychoanalytic Study of the Double in
  Literature.* Wayne State University Press: Detroit, 1970.

Selected Critical Readings:
Heath, Stephen, *"Psychopathia sexualis: Stevenson's Strange
  Case"* in Colin MacCabe (ed), *Futures for English.* Manchester
  University Press, 1988.
Hirsch, Gordon & Veeder, William, *Dr Jekyll and Mr Hyde After
  One Hundred Years.* Chicago University Press, 1986.
Hubbard, Tom, *Seeking Mr Hyde.* Peter Lang: Frankfurt am
  Main, 1995.
Jefford, Andrew, "Dr Jekyll and Professor Nabokov: Reading a
  Reading" in Andrew Noble (ed), *Robert Louis Stevenson.*

The Master of Ballantrae
Edition:
The Master of Ballantrae edited by Emma Letley. Oxford
  University Press, 1983.

Selected Critical Readings:
Bonds, Robert E., "The Mystery of *The Master of Ballantrae"* in
  English Literature in Transition (1964).
Gifford, Douglas, "Stevenson and Scottish Fiction: *The
  Importance of The Master of Ballantrae"* in Jenni Calder (ed),
  Stevenson and Victorian Scotland.
Kilroy, James F., "Narrative Techniques in *The Master of
  Ballantrae"* in *Studies in Scottish Literature* V (1969).
Mills, Carol, *"The Master of Ballantrae:* An Experiment with
  Genre" in Andrew Noble (ed), *Robert Louis Stevenson.*

The Ebb-Tide
Editions:
The Ebb-Tide: A Trio and Quartette in South Sea Tales edited by
  Roslyn Jolly. Oxford University Press, 1996. Quotations in the
  foregoing are from this edition.
[I have silently changed the erroneous 'hutch' to 'hatch' in the
  quotation taken from p.201 of this edition.]

Robert Louis Stevenson and Lloyd Osbourne, *The Ebb-Tide: A Trio and a Quartette* edited by Peter Hinchcliffe and Catherine Kerrigan. Edinburgh University Press, 1994.

It is worth noting the most thorough modern edition which not only restores the full-title on the cover of the book and makes other well-judged textual emendations but also gives some credit to Osbourne for his undoubted, though far from major, input to the writing of the novel.

Selected Critical Readings:

Fowler, Alastair, "Parables of Adventure: The Debatable Novels of Robert Louis Stevenson" in Ian Campbell (ed), *Nineteenth-Century Scottish Fiction: Critical Essays.* Carcanet: Manchester, 1979.

Ricks, Christopher, "A Note on 'The Hollow Men' and Stevenson's *The Ebb-Tide*" in *Essays in Criticism LI* (January 2001), No.1.